STITCH BY STITCH

Copy and Translation of a Convention made in about the Year 1160 between The Dean and Canons of the Church of St. Martin's-le-Grand and The Guild of Saddlers.

STITCH BY STITCH

A GUIDE TO EQUINE SADDLES

COMPANION VOLUME
TO
BIT BY BIT

by

DIANA TUKE

ILLUSTRATED WITH
PHOTOGRAPHS BY
DONALD TUKE

J. A. ALLEN & CO. LTD.
LONDON

British Library Cataloguing in Publication Data

Tuke, Diana
Stitch by stitch,
1, Saddlery
I. Title
685'. 1
TS1032

ISBN 0-85131-049-4

First published 1970
Reprinted 1988

Published in Great Britain by
J. A. Allen & Company Limited
1 Lower Grosvenor Place, Buckingham Palace Road
London SW1W 0EL

Printed and bound in Great Britain by
WBC Bristol & Maesteg

CONTENTS

Books by the same Author

A LONG ROAD TO HARRINGAY – CASSELL & CO. LTD. 1960

BIT BY BIT – J. A. ALLEN & CO. LTD. 1965

ILLUSTRATIONS

Frontispiece: The earliest document referring to the Saddler's Company

CHAPTER THREE – PART II

CHAPTER FOUR

CHAPTER SIX

CONCLUSION

Dedicated to THE WORSHIPFUL COMPANY OF SADDLERS – and all those who have helped with the writing, not only of STITCH-BY-STITCH, but also its companion, BIT-BY-BIT, and without whose help and expert knowledge neither could have been written.

ACKNOWLEDGEMENTS

ACKNOWLEDGEMENTS and grateful thanks are due to the following.

The Worshipful Company of Saddlers, for permission to photograph and reproduce their Crest and ancient Document, and the set of tools on loan from the Museum of Leathercraft – who also granted permission – which were originally displayed at the Great Exhibition of 1851. (Cover, frontispiece and fig. 79.)

Messrs. Grant Barnes and Son, of The Horsefair, Malmesbury, Wiltshire, for their help – loaning us saddles and other items of saddlery for Chapter Five, and giving us the run of the shop for photographing.

Major-General John Bowring, C.B., C.B.E., M.C., and Mrs. Bowring, of Upper House, Chedglow, Crudwell, Malmesbury, Wiltshire, for allowing their eldest daughter to take part – and Caroline for doing so; and letting us use their hunter, Gundulf, and pony, Cloudy, in Chapter Five.

Brigadier John Clabby, O.B.E., M.R.C.V.S., of the Animal Health Trust, 14 Ashley Place, Westminster, London, for obtaining the special photographs.

Mr. L. Constance, M.R.C.V.S., of Kingsmead, Didmarton, Badminton, Gloucestershire, for his help with Chapters Two and Six, especially the latter.

Mr. W. Donaldson, of the Easton Grey Stables, Easton Grey, Malmesbury, Wiltshire, for letting us use the hunter, Myth, and the pony, Sparky.

Messrs. Eldonian (Saddlery and Leather Goods) Ltd., of the Eldonian Works, Bath Street, Walsall, Staffordshire, for their help with Chapters One and Three, and for letting us photograph their works in action and their saddlery.

Messrs. W. & H. Gidden Ltd., of 74 New Oxford Street, London, for letting us photograph some of their saddles.

Captain E. Hartley Edwards, M.C., Editor of *Riding*, of 189 High Holborn, London, for his help and introductions.

Messrs. W. G. Hayes and Son Ltd., of 6 and 8 Dyer Street, Market Place, Cirencester, Gloucestershire, for letting us photograph in their workshop.

Messrs. Hermès, Sellier, of 24 Faub. St. Honoré, Paris, France, for their help and permission to reproduce photographs of their saddles.

Messrs. A. Pariani, of 20148 Milan, Italy, for their help and permission to reproduce photographs of their saddles.

Messrs. George Parker and Sons (Saddlers) Ltd., of 12 Upper St. Martin's Lane, London, for letting us photograph their saddles and other items of saddlery.

The Daily Telegraph.

The Hide and Allied Trades Improvement Society, of Court Road, Banstead, Surrey, for supplying the photograph for fig. 2 and granting permission for its reproduction.

R.S.P.C.A., for allowing their advertisement to be reproduced – fig. 198.

Professor R. H. Smythe, M.R.C.V.S., for allowing his charts – figs. 16, 17, and 18 to be used.

Messrs. Turf and Travel Ltd., of Gerrards Cross, Buckinghamshire, for letting us photograph their saddles and other items of saddlery.

My brother, Donald, who again undertook all the photography for the book.

D.R.T.

1969

PREFACE

SINCE the publication of BIT-BY-BIT in late December 1965 there have been many requests for another book. Having discovered a little about the complex and fascinating subject, bits and bitting, the obvious answer was a companion volume, STITCH-BY-STITCH, covering the equally interesting and important subject, saddles and saddling. For whether we ride astride or side-saddle, be it hunting, jumping, eventing, showing, polo, dressage, racing, or just plain hacking for pleasure, which includes such pastimes as long-distance riding and trekking, saddles can make or mar not only our pleasure but also our own riding and the performance of our horses. No one type of saddle can cover all these fields, so unless we understand the whys and wherefores of good sound saddling and realize how the horse's conformation and anatomy – and our own – govern the construction of our saddles, we will never obtain the best out of ourselves or our horses.

STITCH-BY-STITCH saw its beginning in early May 1968, but alas, much to my personal regret, Castania, who in the three and a half years she had been home with us had given us another foal and then elected to return to a more active life, was not destined to live long enough to take part as she had done so willingly before. We sadly lost our very gallant little chestnut on June 6th – a month following her twentieth birthday; so ended a wonderful partnership that had spanned, on and off, more than fifteen years. A loyal companion and friend, and the best of rides, Tan, as she was known to her friends, always gave of her best, and her indomitable courage was an inspiration to all who knew her. A great character, she will be remembered with deep affection and tremendous gratitude – for I owe her so much, including my life. Even so, you owe a certain amount of this book to Castania, for it was she who made me look closer at saddlery and realize that a good saddle can make all the difference to one's riding and the performance of one's horse – though it was at Porlock that I first had the pleasure of using a modern spring-tree saddle. Up till then I had, like most riders in their time, used saddles of all descriptions, from the comfortable to the distinctly uncomfortable! Wishing to give us all the greatest possible chance of passing our exams, Major "Paddy" Burke, who was then in charge of Porlock, borrowed four modern saddles from other members of the staff; the difference was quite unbelievable. It was a very kind thought and gesture, for in 1954 modern saddles were still extremely new, and few and far between. If I was in any doubt as to the real benefits of a really good saddle that enables the rider to give of his best, that doubt was dispelled for ever.

I do not for one moment pretend to have included every saddle made – I most certainly have not, for there are many variations of each type on the market to-day –

to cover them all would be wellnigh impossible. Every firm claims to make its particular saddle different; so they do up to a point, but in truth they follow a certain pattern for each given type, and I have endeavoured to cover as many of the conventional types as possible – showing some variations, too; of the rest, well, like bits, they merely are more variations on the same themes. For those who are really interested, collecting saddler's catalogues is extremely enlightning and well worth doing, for they give one a very comprehensive picture of the whole wide range of saddles (fig. 1) now on the market – and other items – available for the rider to choose from. I can browse through them for hours – when I have the time!

Not all saddlers make their own saddles – far from it. Some firms act as agents for the big wholesale firms; while others – especially the small country saddlers, who, owing to pressure of work from making other items of saddlery such as bridles, etc., and repairs, cannot spare the time to make their own saddles – have to have them made for them; these saddles will carry their name, whereas many of the saddles made by the wholesale firms carry their name on the label. For example, our own saddlers in Malmesbury, Grant Barnes and Sons, have their saddles made for them by Butler Bros., of the Triumph Works in Walsall, and the saddles carry the name of Grant Barnes and Sons; though some of Butler Bros.' saddles are sold under their own name, too. Eldonian, on the other hand, stamp their saddles with their name, so one buys an Eldonian saddle. Then we have the firms who both make their own saddles and act as agents for the big wholesale firms, too, who may or may not put their own name on. Again we have the saddlery shops, as against the true saddler, whose saddles come from many types of firms. These stores are springing up around the countryside in large numbers and must not be confused with the genuine saddler who knows his job and takes a pride in his craft. They, in many but not every case, are just sellers of saddles. Lastly, we have the saddler who sells only those saddles made within his own saddler's shop. So, as the reader can see, the rider has a fairly wide choice of saddlers and sellers of saddles to choose from, and therefore must use his own common sense and judgement, in conjunction with the saddler's experienced advice, when buying a saddle. If the rider has had the sense to go to a saddler of national or local repute, then he should be quite safe; do not, though, unless you know the firm, buy through the post, without being able to return the saddle if it is no good. On the other hand, it is quite safe to buy this way if you know the firm, for in many cases this is the only way to obtain a special make of saddle.

Sooner or later the rider, too, will come across certain terms in the saddlery trade that need a little explaining. One of these is "bench-made"; this means that one man has made the saddle through all its stages – though now some of the firms employ women to machine certain parts, while others do it all themselves. Hand-made speaks for itself; in the old days all saddles were hand-made and bench-made, the two terms meaning the same thing. Nowadays, though some saddles are made entirely by hand – even having the traditional set seats – other saddles have certain parts stitched by machine, while retaining their high standard of workmanship; these saddles, too, sometimes have a set seat. Speaking to saddlers, before long the terms "London" and "Walsall" will crop up. "London", generally speaking, means bench-made saddles, whereas "Walsall" denotes factory-made saddles. Walsall, like London is a great centre for the saddlery trade, but not all saddles made in Walsall are mass produced – far from it. Though some most definitely are, others are, like Eldonian's, bench made, with one man making each saddle with the help of some machining being done by women. Saddlers are, of course, found in many towns throughout our land, some of which are world famous for their particular saddles.

In the past some saddlers were household names. Sadly, especially in London, many have been forced to fade out – though if you look they are still to be found. As I write this in February 1969, George Parkers and Sons Ltd., of Upper St. Martin's Lane, W.C.2, are as far as I can discover the only firm still carrying on, as they have done since 1851. W. & H. Giddens, of New Oxford Street, W.C.1, who themselves have been in their premises for ninety-seven years and have given a home to such well-known names as Champion & Wilton in 1961 – who had already taken over the old-established firm of Whippy, Staggall & Co., dating from 1786 and also Owen, who had taken over McDougall before going to live with Giddens in 1958. J. I. Sowter & Co. in 1967 returned almost to their original site, when they went to live with Harry Hall at Austin Reed in Regent Street, so, as we can see, though no longer in their own homes in many cases, these old firms whose names were the hall-mark of good saddles are still to be found, and I trust will continue to be for many years to come. Not that many other firms up and down the country do not make first-class saddles, too – they most certainly do – but tradition is worth preserving. While we have our excellent saddles, we also have some that have no right to the name at all, for they are a disgrace, and I hope this book will help the reader to be a little clearer about the subject and be more able to distinguish between the good and the bad.

Spring 1969   D.R.T.

Fig. 1. Saddles of different types.

CHAPTER ONE

FROM TANNERY TO TRADE –
HOW LEATHER IS PRODUCED

LEATHER, as we know it, has come a long way and been through a great many processes since its original state. Hence the reason why good leather, and therefore good, reliable saddlery, can never be cheap.

Nevertheless, good leather has its own reward, for not only does it last far, far longer than cheap, poor-quality stuff, but there is something extremely satisfying about the feel and look of the really top-quality variety.

Treated fairly, and well cared for, it will last a lifetime and prove far less expensive in the long run – besides, cheap leather is dangerous, it can and does break without warning. So if you value your life and your horse, buy only the best and then look after it – for starved leather can also break!

In order to appreciate our saddles and get the best out of them for our own comfort and also that of our horses, it is necessary to first know a little about leather – where it comes from and how it is produced.

Leather, as most of us know, comes from animal skins: hides as they are called in the case of bovine skins – in other words those of cattle. Hides make up the biggest percentage of skins used in the saddlery trade and must be of the highest quality. The best ones come from slow-maturing cattle, as they must have time to thicken, and in particular the Aberdeen Angus.

England cannot produce nearly enough hides to satisfy the enormous demand of the saddlery trade, so in order to try to keep pace with saddlers and their ever-increasing demand a large number of hides have to be imported in the rough – that is after they have been tanned, but before being curried, as the art of currying in this country is the most highly developed in the world and second to none.

Where bovine hides amount to about 90 per cent of the hides used in the saddlery trade, pigskin, used in covering the seats of saddles and sometimes the flaps in expensive saddles, doeskin, also used for some seats and flaps, besides knee grips on those saddles that have them, and sheepskin, which, reversed, is used to back saddle panels and line cheaper ones, also all play their part and make up the remaining 10 per cent. Sheepskin in this respect is known as basil, and is the sheepskin less the wool.

One important factor in favour of imported hides is the fact that they are freer from warble holes and wire scars, both of which are rife in our home-produced hides and a serious problem; America, too, suffers in the same way and the wastage is very great, as the control of warbles is not as good as it should be and barbed wire is used so extensively in our modern age.

What is a warble? Well, it is a small fat maggot that has spent the previous winter and late summer growing and travelling within its "host" – cattle and horses both suffer from warbles – but more about them later on in relation to the horse itself. During the winter, towards the spring, a small swelling can be felt under the skin, which shifts from place to place for a time before settling down in one spot. The larva then bores itself a tiny hole in the skin, through which to breathe. Here it lives, growing fat and causing a larger and larger swelling on the animal's back. Some badly infected cattle are a solid mass of lumps all over their backs. Once "ripe" the larva pops out through its breathing hole – suitably enlarged to let it free (fig. 2) – and falls to the ground and pupates. Several weeks later the adult fly emerges – the *Hypoderma bovis*. This fly then in its turn lays its eggs on the hair of its "host" in sunny weather – several eggs to a hair. Having hatched out at the roots of the hair, in the open air, a few days after being laid, the grub quickly bores himself a tiny hole into the skin of its "host" and enters the connective tissue (usually in the region of the hind quarters), where, in some unknown manner, it travels through the tissue to reach the animal's back, where it forms the warble lump as we see it, with its tiny breathing hole.

If during a hot sunny day we see cattle galloping around a field with their tails aloft, ten to one the warble fly is after its victim to ensure a winter's billet! Unfortunately the hole made in the hide by the larva when it settles on the cattle's back renders that part of the hide useless in the trade for good-quality saddlery. These hides are extremely wasteful and uneconomical to cut and have to be avoided where possible, making unmarked hides all that more expensive.

Wire marks, too, cause a serious problem, as they can disfigure the leather and render it fit only for less expensive saddles, where a few marks have to be accepted. To find hides free of marks is extremely difficult – especially home-produced ones – for if one watches cattle out in a field before long they will find themselves a rubbing post of some sort; a wire fence or a tree with a good "itching point" are firm favourites – they positively enjoy themselves rubbing their necks and backs as hard as they can; unfortunately, those hides will be of little use for top-quality saddlery!

If one looks at the leather lining of a new saddle, one will see, especially on the less expensive ones, thin scratches; these are wire marks that have healed, forming scars. In the best-quality saddles the saddler tries to use leather as blemish free as possible, and I personally would never buy a saddle with a panel badly blemished, for it is unsightly to say the least of it – though some people do accept wire marks. On saddle flaps it is possible to emboss the marks out when the pigskin grain is embossed on to the leather to make it look like pigskin – for except in very light racing saddles, in the quest for extreme lightness, pigskin is not normally used for saddle flaps. In the past, and occasionally now, expensive saddles do have their flaps covered with pigskin. In the same way as they are covered in doeskin and brushed pigskin (the grain side is brushed) today.

So much for choosing the hides; now we will look briefly – for leather-making is a lengthy business requiring many machines and processes – at the art of tanning and currying, and the different parts of the hide once it has been cut up ready for the trade.

The art of tanning is very old indeed and its object is to cure the hides and render them imperishable. In all probability early man started to tan leather by accident, for like so many important discoveries – it just happened. In the case of tanning it is thought that man left a skin in a puddle full of bits of tree and unknowingly tanned it, for tree bark, etc., contains tannin or tannic acid, which will convert animal skins into leather. In the ensuing years man became more experienced and leather-making was an important trade among the ancient Egyptians, who used it for harness, besides other things. By the time the Romans invaded Britain the art of leather-making was an important trade in our land, too, for we had the great oak trees whose bark contains quite a lot of tannic acid. Today, oak-bark tanning is still considered one of the best and is carried on in modern buildings with up-to-date know-how and mechanical devices; all the same, the basic oak-bark tanning is the same as it was in those far-off days of early man.

When the raw skins come into the tanneries they have to be cleansed first of dirt, salt, etc., which is done by washing them in clean water. The hides are then transferred to pits in which lime has been dissolved. The main object of soaking the hides in lime is to loosen the hair, but it has other equally important uses; for the swelling that is caused separates the fibre bundles into their constituent fibrils and so increases the fullness and pliability of the leather.

After about ten days in the lime pits, the hides are ready to have the hair and flesh removed; this is done by a big machine. The hides now look more like hides as we know them and have the familiar grain – that is the side which contained the hair – and the flesh side, which speaks for itself. It is very important to remember which side is which, for with our tack it is the flesh side that should receive the greater part of the oil and greasing to keep it soft and supple, and in safe, good condition. In other words, it is the flesh side, like the underside of a saddle flap (fig. 3), that must be fed – the grain side is merely cleaned and preserved. As the flesh side is normally on the inside, and therefore out of sight, it is the side the lazy and ignorant are most prone to leave, which is why so much good tack is ruined annually. The next step is for the hides to be thrown back into cold water ready for scudding and rounding. In the old days scudding was done by hand, the hide being placed over a beam and a blunt knife used to squeeze and push the grain to remove loose protein, hair roots, gland tissue, pigment and some loose fat, all of which is commonly known as scud. Nowadays, scudding is mostly done by machine. Rounding, though, is still a hand process. The hides are sorted and their future determined – the best, with the most substance, going to the saddlery trade and other industries requiring top-quality leather. Those hides that are to be cut up at this stage are placed on a table and a rounding frame on top of them; otherwise, they are tanned whole and then rounded before being curried, which we will hear about later.

The lime, having served its purpose of loosening the hair, must now be removed, prior to the actual tanning. Tanning can either be done by a vegetable process – which is why in the old days tanneries were found near to big oak woods, like Sherwood Forest, so that the oak bark used in tanning was readily available – or by mineral tannage, in minerals such as alum salts; for thousands of years man has used the salts of aluminium to tan leather, and, after trying other minerals without much success, hit on the salts of chromium in the nineteenth century, producing what we know as chrome-tanned leather. It was Augustus Schultz, an American chemist, who first developed chrome-tanned leather, but his was, though very resistant to water and more quickly produced than other kinds of leather, extremely hard and unyielding, of a blue colour. Nothing daunted, they soldiered on, and in the end a young Philadelphian tanner, Robert Foerderer, discovered that he could make it soft and pliable by the use of soap and oil, so thanks to these two men, and many more, we have today chrome leather that will withstand wet and retain its suppleness. Tanning, as is generally known, is the actual conversion of the hides into leather. In vegetable tanning the hides go into suspenders – a series of eight to ten deep pits through which they pass, before being laid away; that is, stacked in pits one on top of the other, where they remain for some weeks. After which time they are removed and the tanning liquid – known as "liquor" – replaced by a new lot and the hides returned to remain there for some months. On the completion of this process they are removed from the pits for finishing. Great care must be taken at this stage, which consists of oiling, rolling and drying. All this takes time and cannot be hurried. The hides have to be dried at an even temperature and without any sudden draughts which can and will mark them by scorching. If one studies a hide closely in the rough, it will be found to have brown crinkly edges, and this brown staining can spread over quite a large area. One hide I saw was stained over about a third of its grain side; evidently the hide had accidentally been left in a draught during drying.

The next stage is currying – an ancient craft dating back to the fourteenth century. At a slightly later date it was admitted to the craft guilds.

The object of currying is to dress the leather. Few saddlery firms now curry their own leather – though the firm I visited still has its own currying shop, and is, I believe, unique in this respect. Most saddlers purchase their leather in the finished state, that is curried, the currying having been done in all probability by a firm which also tans leather. The saddler has the choice of purchasing either a full hide, a half hide, or side, which means it has been split down the backbone from shoulder to tail, or back, which is the half hide minus the belly (fig. 4), which is the thinner piece that comes underneath. Alternatively, the hide can be cut in the following way: shoulder, the bit across the top; butts, the best bit and the same as the back, but not necessarily split down the backbone, and again belly. To cut the hide this way the full hide (fig. 5) is placed on a table and on top of it a rounding-off frame measuring 5 feet by 4 feet, to indicate where to cut the hide. First the bellies are removed from either side; then the shoulder from across the top: this leaves the best and most prized bit of the hide – the butts. The best of all goes to make bridles and the next for saddles. Hence the reason why warbles damage the hides so. Panel hides are left whole and the flesh side is not flattened down, for it is always on the inside and out of sight – which is why they look rough on the flesh side, whereas other leather used in the saddlery trade should look and feel absolutely smooth in texture, for rough, loose fibres should not be tolerated in top-quality leather. Too, a panel hide should be as blemish free as possible.

When selecting a hide (fig. 6) substance has to be taken into consideration; this is extremely important. For substance means strength. More weight – more substance. A 30 lb. back will go to make saddle flaps, or a 20 lb. butt for the top-grade ones. In cheaper saddles shoulder is used, but it is coarser and more prone to scratches. The thicker the leather, too, the more fat it will hold and therefore the greater its strength

Having selected the hide or parts of the hide required from the warehouse (fig. 7), where the hides from the tannery have been stored (in the case of a firm like this that has its own currying shop), for they can buy leather in the rough, the next step is to take it and put it into vats of water overnight. It is surprising how much scum comes to the surface of the water during the night. From the vats they are taken and put through a large splitting machine to reduce them to an even thickness, as no hide is the same thickness all over. Sometimes only the tiniest sliver comes off and at others quite a sizeable piece. From the splitting machine they pass to the shaving machine, which can be controlled to a fine degree (fig. 8). The object of this is to reduce the leather to the required substance. This finished, they return to the vats for another three to four days.

Next they have to be cleaned to rid them of all bacteria and other unwanted things; for this they are put into large revolving drums that have wooden slats on the inside that beat the leather as it falls against it. If one has ever used a drier in a launderette and watched blankets, etc., going round and round inside the drums, then one can picture the bits of leather in the revolving drums, reaching the roof and falling back to the bottom again, hitting the sides as they go. These drums contain acids to start with, and then plain, clean water, to wash out the acids.

Slicking out comes next, a process by which the water is removed. Then, while still damp, they have a hand setting machine passed over them. The leather is placed on a table and the machine pushed to and fro across the surface to push it out, and in doing so, it flattens out a great number of the natural growth marks.

According to the ultimate use of the leather, the number of processes through which it passes during currying varies slightly. I have only gone into those applicable to the saddlery trade.

The leather is now said to be in the russet stage and is hung up overnight on big frames by toggles (fig. 9) – special clips like large clothes pegs. In this photograph we have a shoulder being fastened to the frames, and underneath the big pipes that supply the heat to dry the hides can be clearly seen. The temperature is quite high and in the summer can become fairly stuffy – in winter no doubt it is cosy! Once dry they are removed and pass on to the buffing machine. On good saddlery leather very little buffing is done; it is better to leave a few small scratches than to spoil the character and real strength of the leather by trying to remove them.

The colour of the leather is decided on next, London being usually the light finish, Havana the colour of a good cigar, and Warwick much darker. While in the fancy-leather trade some leather, where the colour has to be right through, is dyed in vats, in the saddlery trade the colour is normally applied by pad staining – that is, the dye is applied by means of a soft pad of cloth or something similar. In both trades dye is also sprayed on in some instances. Though it is usual in the saddlery trade to colour leather some shade of brown, of course, black leather is used, too. In America black saddles are becoming the fashion on grey horses for some special show classes. I have seen several destined for the American market in different saddlers this summer. One even had black patent leather flaps; this is an exception, certainly not the rule!

When the dye is dry the leather is then passed through the plating machine (fig. 10); the object of this is to flatten the leather, as can be seen in the photograph, and where grain is required it is then embossed on before going through to the greasing department (fig. 11). Here the nature is put back into the leather by means of a mixture of tallow and cod's oil. In the forefront of the photograph the glazing machine can be seen, while in the background on the right the butts (fig. 12) awaiting their turn to be greased. Both sides are done and in the good old-fashioned way (figs. 13 and 14) – by hand, using a pad of soft cloth and one's arm. The grain is done first and then the flesh side, making quite sure plenty is applied. Stirrup leathers are done twice.

It takes around three weeks to pass through the currying shop, and curriers like to keep the finished leather for a while after that to mature. The demand for leather nowadays for the saddlery trade is so great that it is hard to keep pace – often the cupboard is bare (fig. 15)! Nevertheless the curriers do an excellent job and keep pace fairly well.

When we come to choose saddlery it is essential to know how we can tell if it has been made in good leather or not, for though we will be guided by our saddler it is up to us to use our own judgement, too. Good leather should have plenty of substance and the flesh side should be smooth in texture with no loose or rough fibres visible – though this does not apply to the flesh side of a panel hide, as this has not been plated; should the leather be a mass of loose fibres, then leave it alone. The same applies if it is dry – good leather should be both greasy in appearance and feel; if one looks at new leather in a saddler's store room, it often has a greyish tinge over it – this is grease, and is excellent. But above all else leather must be firm and on no account should it feel pappy when handled. Good leather when bent by hand, though it will wrinkle naturally, will show no signs of bubbling either on the grain side or the flesh side and return to normal when released and straightened out again.

The next thing, having chosen one's saddlery in the best leather available, is to look after it so as to ensure that it lasts its full span of life – which is very many years. Saddlery should if possible be kept in an even temperature – neither too hot nor too cold or damp; ordinary room temperature is about right. When not in use it is best to cover one's saddle either with a cloth or a proper cover to keep off the dust. Unfortunately leather is rather susceptible to scratching, so care must be exercised to ensure that irrevocable damage is not done to a good saddle by careless handling. When saddling up or unsaddling it as well to place the saddle well out of harm's way both from the horse and oneself – it is so easy to step back unwittingly on one's saddle or for one's horse to do so; but above all one must refrain from flinging a saddle down just anywhere – if one cannot remove it from the box, then it must be placed in a safe corner either on a rug or straw, or if one is outside, on grass, taking care not to prop it up against a rough wall, as this is how the cantle gets damaged by either scratching or even cutting Many people place their saddle on the stable door; this, if the lining is either of serge or linen, is reasonably safe, providing it does not get knocked off, but a leather lining would be marked, unless, of course, there was a stable rug hanging over the door to place it on.

Cleaning saddlery is well worth the time spent, as both the horse and the leather benefit from it. In the former's case dirt only causes trouble, whereas with the latter the time spent ensures its long life and safety. Whatever one uses to clean and preserve one's leather, the leather must be first thoroughly cleaned – care being taken to remove all the mud and dried sweat marks. I find a piece of towelling or a face cloth quick and efficient for this, and wrung out frequently in clean water it will remove all the dirt without just smearing it around. When cleaning leather care must be taken not to have the water too hot; this only removes too much oil from the leather, leaving it dry. A well-wrung cloth, I find, does not wet the leather, but merely damps it, so that one can wipe it dry when one has finished. Once clean, the saddle soap or other dressing can be applied. For every day care I rely on a first-class glycerine saddle soap, as I find this does not clog up the leather and really cleans and preserves, so that the leather keeps soft and supple, as it should. Most people use a large sponge for saddle soap, but I have found a flat "Spontex Moppet" far quicker and handier to use, as it folds easily round the straps, and for large areas like saddle flaps whips over the surface in no time if well charged with soap and used in a circular motion to work the soap well into the leather. I have used a moppet now for about four years and would not return to a proper-sized sponge. Cheap, they can be renewed without hurting one's purse! Sometimes small accumulations of grease build up on the leather — known as jockeys; these should be removed before soaping, either with a matchstick used on its side or with a blunt knife, care being taken not to scratch the surface of the leather. Though if one cleans one's tack every time it is used — as it should be — then these jockeys do not normally build up, and if they appear they will wipe off in the course of cleaning.

Though saddle soap will keep leather soft and supple, it is not sufficient on its own to replace the nature lost from the leather during everyday use — some other type of leather dressing is needed in addition. Principally two things remove the nature — one is heat and the other is wet. The former is generated by the horse's body when in work, which tends to dry out the leather; as will drying wet leather that has come in soaked with rain or sweat — or both — in front of a hot fire or over hot pipes. Leather must be dried slowly at room temperature, otherwise it will crack and then break. Once dry, the nature should be put back by the use of some reliable leather dressing — Kocholine is hard to beat and Flexalan is another widely used preparation though, there are others — but whatever is used it should be applied to the flesh side and worked in with one's fingers. Well-cared-for leather, as I said earlier, should be soft and supple, but this does not mean soggy. Over oiling can lead to this and can be just as harmful as underfeeding, for leather is able to hold only a certain amount of oil; over do it and it will all ooze out again, which is bad not only for the horse's skin but also for one's clothes. In this respect neatsfoot oil is a sinner — excellent in itself, it must be used with discretion. In the old days nothing else was used, as far as I know, and many people still use it — I for one, but only about once a year when I give my tack a special doing. In the usual run of things I use Kocholine at regular intervals — with saddle soap every day — and normally only saddle soap on the parts of the saddle that come in contact with one's clothes; otherwise they get stained. Too, as the grain side is partly sealed, there is little point in putting dressing on this side, as it cannot soak in so easily as it does on the flesh side, that is not sealed.

So much for leather. From tannery to trade takes time, and as a great deal of it is hand work — manpower. Nevertheless, good leather is worth buying and provided it is looked after — worth the money spent.

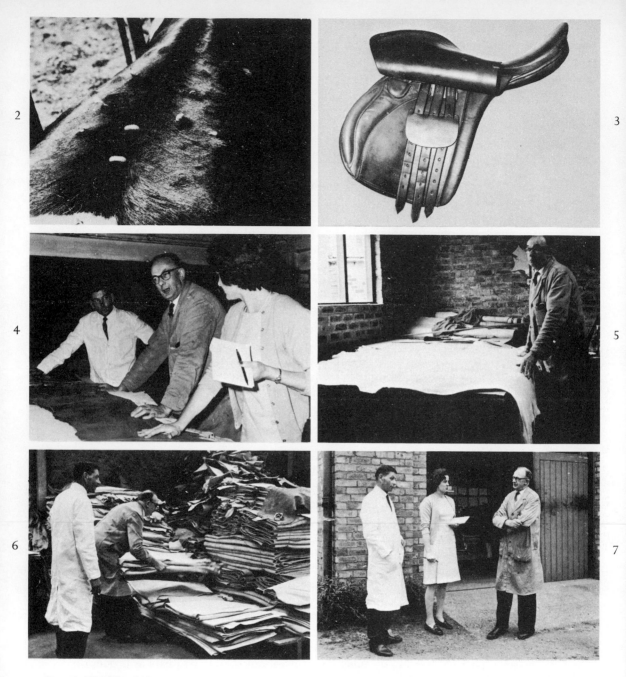

Fig. 2. Warble lumps – and "ripe" larvae emerging.

Fig. 4. Belly.

Fig. 6. Selecting a hide.

Fig. 3. The flesh side, like the underside of a saddle flap (66).

Fig. 5. Full hide.

Fig. 7. The warehouse where the hides from the tanneries are stored.

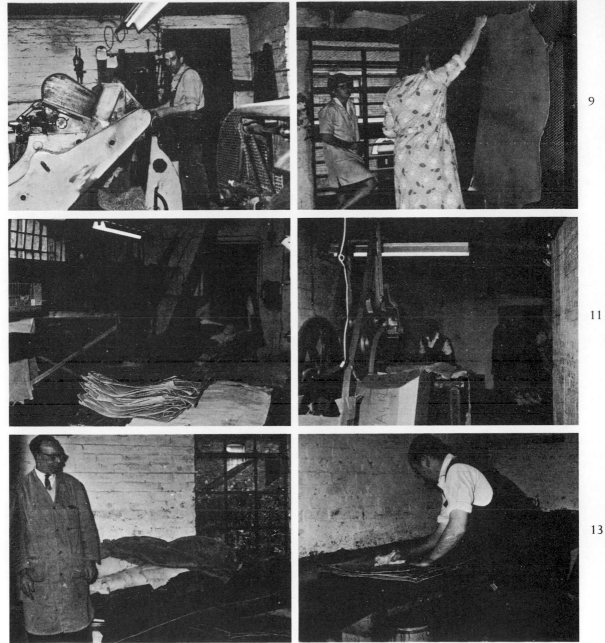

Fig. 8. The shaving machine.
Fig. 10. The plating machine.
Fig. 12. A butt waiting to be greased.

Fig. 9. Hanging up by toggles to dry.
Fig. 11. The greasing department – glazing machine in foreground.
Fig. 13. Greasing – in the good old fashioned way.

14   15

Fig. 14. Greasing – in the good old fashioned way.

Fig. 15. It is hard to keep pace – often the cupboard is bare.

CHAPTER TWO

AN INTRODUCTION TO THE ART OF SADDLING

THE equine saddle dates back many hundreds of years, but not so many as the equine bit. Originally man rode either bareback or on a blanket, and only later started using a saddle. Even so, that is an extremely long time ago and the saddle has come a long way since those far-off times. Like bits, saddles became very ornate, heavy affairs, and coupled with the armour worn by both man and his horse constituted a considerable weight for the horse to carry. Mercifully that age passed and the horse had only his rider and saddle to carry; nevertheless, it was still far greater than the weight we expect our horses to carry today. If one studies old paintings, it is extremely interesting to see how through the years the saddle changes, till by the late 1700s and early 1800s they had become remarkably like our old type of hunting saddle. John Ferneley (1782–1860), in his sketch for the Belvoir Hunt picture signed and dated 1823, and Henry Alken, sen. (1774–1850), in his famous painting "The Meet", both depict saddles closely akin to prewar hunting saddles, though with a straighter flap and seat than we normally have today, for it was the custom to use a much straighter leg and therefore longer leather. At the turn of the century, thanks largely to Tod Sloan (1874–1933), the American jockey who in 1897 brought the crouching style of race riding with its short leather to our land, and Federico Caprilli (1868–1907), who is the undoubted originator of the modern forward seat, which was introduced to the riding world by this Italian cavalry officer in 1890, and known since 1907 as the Italian or forward seat, things began to change, though only very slowly. With the advent of the shorter leather and the forward seat it became necessary to alter the shape of the saddle to enable the rider to adopt this style of riding. Though to a certain extent the old type of saddle is still to be found (and treasured by some), and in a moderated form sought after by a fairly large number of riders, the modern saddle, built to enable the rider to get the best out of themselves and their horses, with far greater security for the rider and degree of comfort for both, is now the most favoured, and quite rightly so.

The type of saddle we buy depends largely on the particular sport or pastime we wish to partake in, but whatever type of saddle we choose we must first consider our horse's anatomy and how it affects the whole aspect of saddling, for not only does it influence the fit of the saddle, and therefore the horse's comfort and our own, but also its construction. To appreciate this it is essential to know a little about what lies beneath the saddle.

If we study the following diagrams (figs. 16, 17 and 18) showing the bones, points and muscles of the horse and compare them against the accompanying photograph of Castania (fig. 19) – taken incidentally in the March before she died – we will get a fair picture of what we are talking about.

Taking the bone structure first, it is the dorsal and lumbar vertebrae, the ribs, the sternum (or breast-bone) and the scapula (or shoulder blade) with which we are concerned, for these are the bones most directly involved in saddling. Even so, we must first take a quick look at the spinal column as a whole to appreciate the section we are interested in. It consists of seven cervical vertebrae – or neck bones; eighteen dorsal vertebrae, to which are joined the ribs – a pair to each bone; six lumbar vertebrae (in some breeds of Eastern origin like the Arab there may only be five lumbar vertebrae, in which case there will be an extra dorsal vertebra) – these form the loins; the sacrum – which is made up of five bones fused together by ossification of the cartilaginous material that united them in their foetal stage; the centre of these four groups of vertebrae are hollow, and form the neural canal – the channel through which runs the spinal cord to terminate in the middle of the sacrum, from whence it gives off nerves to serve the coccygeal vertebrae (or tail), which completes the spinal column.

As far as the saddle itself is concerned, this is placed over the dorsal vertebrae that accommodate the heads of the last ten pairs of ribs – the false ribs as they are often known as – the last of which is not joined to its predecessor as in the case of the other nine pairs, but is free and therefore known as a "floating rib". Having the ribs to support it, this section of the spine is very strong, whereas if we move our weight back beyond the last dorsal vertebra we put it over the lumbar vertebrae that form merely a bridge of bone between the ribs and the pelvis, and therefore very much weaker in consequence. The shape of the dorsal vertebrae is of the greatest importance, for it determines the construction of the saddle. Unlike the common conception, the backbone of the horse is not flat – rather it is shaped like an inverted T. The dorsal vertebrae are squarish bones with a fin-like piece of bone rising from the centre of each – the spinal process. In the early vertebrae these spinous processes form the withers and determine their height, being of great length, though their length varies from horse to horse. This is the reason why horses' withers vary in height, some having far higher withers than others. The spinal process is also the reason why our saddles have to be made with a gullet (fig. 20) – the gap between the two sides of the panel – for they measure approximately $2\frac{1}{2}$ inches square across their heads, and should the horse be in poor condition, so that the edges are not protected by muscle, they can be injured by pressure or pinching if the gullet is not wide enough.

It is the ribs, though, that bear our weight where they articulate with the dorsal vertebrae. These ribs are elongated, curved and highly elastic bones, which at their lower end carry a prolongation in the form of a rod of cartilage. In older horses the cartilage calicifies and becomes solid, but in younger ones this is not so – they are soft and composed of gristle. Both the length of the ribs and their spring or curve varies, and is of importance both from the point of view of saddling and also performance. A horse that lacks sufficient spring will be hard to saddle, as the saddle will be for ever sliding to the rear, whereas one with a well-sprung rib cage will keep his saddle in the correct place and be far more comfortable to ride into the bargain. The first eight pairs of ribs – the true ribs – are not normally so curved as the last ten pairs; ideally the ribs should increase in spring as they travel back towards the last, which should have the greatest spring. The rib cage also contains the lungs and heart, and each time the horse breathes, by virtue of the muscles that lie between and overlie them, the ribs rotate. In a forward direction when he takes in air, thereby increasing the capacity of the chest (hence the reason a horse can blow itself out just when we wish to girth up), and in the opposite direction when he breathes out – the ribs then lie flat against the chest to force out the air from the lungs. For this reason a horse should never be girthed up too tight; room must be left for the horse to expand and thereby gain enough air in his lungs to enable him to perform his work to the best of his ability.

Moving down from the ribs we come to the sternum; this bone forms the floor of the chest – or thorax and joins the ends of the first eight pairs of ribs. The groove formed at the termination of this bone provides a convenient solid piece of bone over which to place the girth and hold it there just behind the elbows, thereby reducing the risk of girthing up too tightly over the softer cartilage of the other ribs – though this is not so necessary with mature horses as it is with immature ones.

Lastly we come to the scapula, which of all the bones varies more in length from horse to horse than any other. The slope of the shoulder is determined by this bone, as it is always attached to the same dorsal spines – the shorter the scapula the straighter the shoulder, especially if the spinous processes are not very long. The longer the spines the greater the angle of obliqueness, as the blade is carried further back; this makes for a good shoulder behind which the saddle can rest comfortably without interfering with the action of the shoulder. The scapula in its turn is attached to the spine by its cartilage of prolongation, by means of muscles and ligaments; for, unlike, us the horse has no collar-bone.

So much for the framework of the horse. We turn now to the muscles that play an equally important part in saddling. Comparing figs. 18 and 19, we can see how the external layer of muscles lie. Castania had been up all winter, and though in big condition was pretty hard and fit. A fit horse is one that is well muscled up, whereas a fat horse is soft and unfit for any but very slow work. Though some horses when fit and hard are lean, this is not always the case; some carry a reasonable amount of flesh, but are equally fit and hard. One must distinguish, too, between the horse in big hard condition and its brother in fat soft condition; the same way as one must between the horse trained off light, but is fighting fit, and its opposite number who is merely in poor condition. Owing to its make-up, a horse must have its muscles well developed – a horse with good strong muscles will be far easier to saddle and more comfortable to ride, for it is on the muscles that pack either side of the spinal column, forming a sort of protection pad, that we place our saddles. Too, with well-developed muscles the risk of injury is greatly reduced – a lack of muscles and we find the saddle resting far too close to the bones themselves, with the additional risk of the saddle causing pressure on the spine and also pinching. To convert a soft, flabby horse into a fit hard one, that is well muscled up, needs long hours of steady exercise, increasing in distance and time as the horse gets fitter, coupled with plenty of good protein food in relation to the exercise given – more exercise, more concentrate food – oats, high- or medium-protein horse nuts (the harder the work the higher the protein) and linseed, coupled with good down-to-earth grooming, containing its fair share of sound, sensible strapping to tone up the muscles. Muscles also affect the shape of the withers. In some horses they are so high and lacking in muscles that they stand up in a great half-moon crescent, with a dip where the neck runs into the withers. These withers present their own problem in saddling and great care has to be exercised in choosing a saddle to ensure complete clearance and freedom from interference.

So much for the part the horse's anatomy plays in saddling; we now come to our own – yes, this, too, has a bearing on the subject. As with horses, no two riders are quite alike; even if they are of the same height, build and weight, they may well have legs of different lengths proportionally. It is our legs and build that affect saddling most. With regard to our legs the bones concerned are the femur (or thigh bone), which runs from our pelvis to our knee and lies against the saddle from its twist down to the centre of the flap where the knee roll comes, and the tibia (or shin-bone), that runs from our knee down to our ankle, which joins it to our foot, and rests against the lower part of the saddle flap and then hangs free with the foot resting in the stirrup iron, its contact with the saddle being via the stirrup leather that lies on the inside of the rider's leg. Should the rider have a long thigh-bone, then when the knee is in its correct position on the knee roll of the saddle the rider's pelvis (or seat bones) will have moved further back towards the cantle of the saddle and the horse's loins – for this reason he will require a longer saddle than one with a short thigh-bone. The length of the shin-bone only determines the length of stirrup leather required – which is why two riders of the same overall height may well ride at different lengths using the same saddle. As for our build, the rider who is slimly built can use a saddle that if used by a more heavily built rider would cause a serious risk of injury, for the latter's weight would be on the cantle and very near to, or even over, the horse's loins. In short, our saddles must be built to fit not only the horse but also the rider.

Later on, when we have had time to see how saddles are made, and how they fit, we will look at saddle injuries, though first we must gain a fuller picture to enable us to understand more clearly.

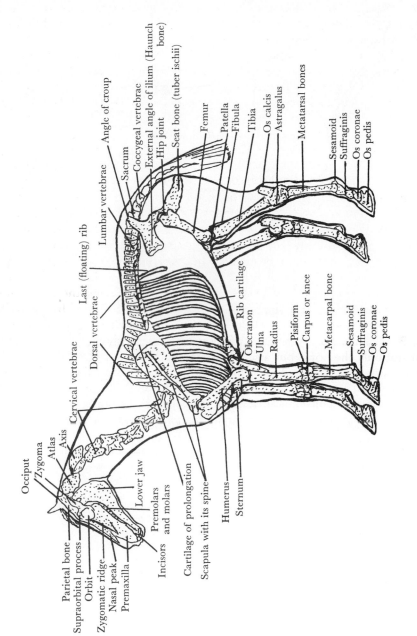

Fig. 16. Anatomical studies – the bones of the horse.

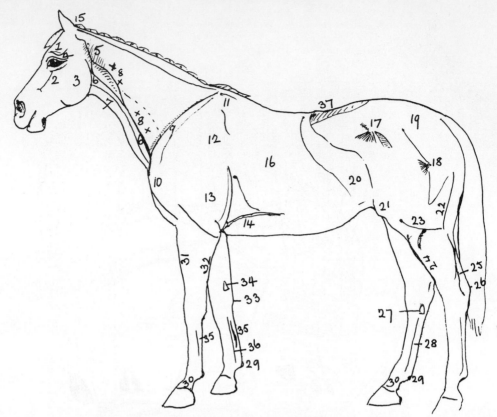

Fig. 17. Anatomical studies – the points of the horse.

(1) *Supraorbital fossa.*
(2) *Zygomatic ridge.*
(3) *Masseter muscle.*
(4) *Supraorbital process.*
(5) *Atlas bone.*
(6) *Jugular furrow.*
(7) *Trachea.*
(8) *Mastoido-humeralis muscle.*
(9) *Supraspinatus muscle.*
(10) *Shoulder joint.*
(11) *Wither.*
(12) *Infraspinatus muscle.*
(13) *Vastus muscles.*
(14) *Spur vein.*
(15) *Poll or occiput.*
(16) *Ribs.*
(17) *Haunch bone.*
(18) *Great trochanter of femur, overlying hip joint.*
(19) *Quarter.*

(20) *Flank.*
(21) *Stifle.*
(22) *Semitendinosus muscle.*
(23) *Biceps femoris muscle.*
(24) *Gaskin or second thigh.*
(25) *Achilles tendon (gastrocnemius).*
(26) *Tuber calcis (point of hock).*
(27) *Chestnut.*
(28) *Flexor tendons.*
(29) *Ergot.*
(30) *Pastern.*
(31) *Forearm (extensor muscles).*
(32) *Forearm (flexor muscles).*
(33) *Pisiform bone.*
(34) *Chestnut.*
(35) *Flexor tendons.*
(36) *Suspensory ligament.*
(37) *Loin.*
(XX XX) *Cervical bones.*

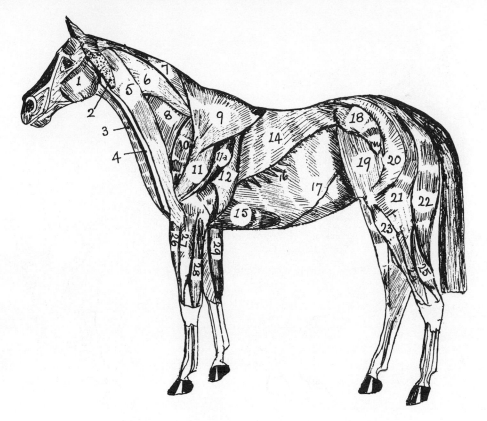

Fig. 18. Anatomical studies – the muscles of the horse.

(1) *Masseter.*
(2) *Parotid gland.*
(3) *Sterno-maxillaris.*
(4) *Jugular furrow.*
(5) *Mastoido-humeralis.*
(6) *Splenius.*
(7) *Rhomboideus.*
(8) *Levator anguli scapulae.*
(9) *Trapezius.*
(10) *Supraspinatus.*
(11) *Infraspinatus* (11a) *Deltoid.*
(12) *Large head of triceps.*
(13) *Middle head of triceps.*
(14) *Latissimus dorsi.*
(15) *Pectoral.*

(16) *Serratus magnus.*
(17) *External oblique.*
(18) *Middle gluteus.*
(19) *Tensor vaginae femoris.*
(20) *Superficial gluteus.*
(21) *Long vastus.*
(22) *Semitendinosus.*
(23) *Extensor pedis.*
(24) *Peroneus.*
(25) *Gastrocnemius.*
(26) *Extensor metacarpi.*
(27) *Extensor pedis.*
(28) *Flexor metacarpi.*
(29) *Flexor metacarpi.*

Fig. 19. Photographic evidence for comparison.

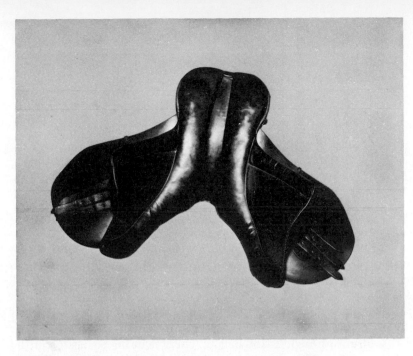

Fig. 20. Saddles have to be made with a gullet (65).

39

CHAPTER THREE

STITCH BY STITCH –
MODERN SADDLES AND HOW THEY ARE MADE

Part One – Saddler's Craft

THE aim of a good saddle is to help position the rider correctly on the horse's back so as to afford him – or her – the maximum security, thereby enabling him to obtain the best out of his mount in his chosen equestrian field. Owing to the diversity of sports in which we partake with our horses. it is impossible for one type of saddle to embrace all the fields – though the basic construction of the different types of saddles is more or less the same.

The art of saddle-making goes back an incredibly long time, and though the exact date of the formation of the Saddler's Company is unknown – lost, no doubt, in antiquity – it is probably of Anglo-Saxon origin. There is in the possession of the Dean and Chapter of Westminster a document showing that it was in existence long before 1160 (Frontispiece). The Great Fire destroyed their first Hall in 1666 and their second went in 1821, while the third, also built on the original site of the previous two, fell victim to the London Blitz in December 1940. The Company now has a new Hall on that site and ranks twenty-fifth in precedence among the City Livery Companies; the Loriner's Company ranks fifty-third and the first known reference to them is in 1245.

Having ascertained a little of the mysteries of leather and how the horse's anatomy and our own govern the construction of the saddle, we will now look closer at this ancient craft and the variety of saddles available for us to choose from.

Saddles, according to the Oxford dictionary, derive their name from the common-Teutonic – namely the Old English – Sadol(ian), the Dutch Sadel(en), and the German Sattel(n), all meaning sit, and fall into three main groups: those built on a full tree (either rigid or spring); those employing only a half tree, and lastly the ones that dispense with a tree altogether. There are, of course, variations within these groups.

The saddler's craft is an extremely interesting one that takes much skill and patience, besides time; therefore, before we go any further into the mysteries of their craft, we must acquaint ourselves with the various points of the saddle and its tree, so as to be conversant with their names. If we study the following three photographs and diagrams (figs. 21, 22 and 23), of a modern, all-purpose saddle, with a continental panel and built on a spring tree with a sloping head and flexible points, and the three of two modern trees (figs. 24, 25 and 26), one spring and the other rigid, both destined to have flexible points (i.e. leather points), we will then know what is what.

Trees, as we know, are the basic foundation of a saddle and both the rigid and spring ones start life in the same way. The spring tree is of fairly recent origin. In the old days trees were made by hand out of beechwood, nowadays the majority are made out of laminated wood — though other materials have been used with varying degrees of success. In order to achieve the correct shape a mould is made and on it the wooden framework is built up from pre-cut pieces of beech veneers. This done, the laminations are then bonded together under heat and pressure with urea formaldehyde resin, which produces a frame of considerable strength and durability, and a great deal lighter than the old type of solid beechwood tree. For this reason, too, they do not break quite so easily as the old type. The next stage is for the framework to be covered with muslin and a water-resistant coating to increase its strength and give it extra resistance to moisture. Even so, the wooden frame on its own would not be strong enough to withstand the stress and strain imposed on it by rider and horse alike, so in order to overcome this steel plates — or in some cases Duralumin (dura-aluminium), giving extra lightness while retaining strength — are riveted on to the frame to reinforce it, as we saw in figs. 24, 25 and 26. In rigid trees and spring ones we have the gullet plate — a specially shaped steel plate that goes on the underside of the pommel — and the head plate that goes over the top. These are joined by rivets fitted by hand. Another plate is then riveted to the underside of the cantle. In the rigid tree this is a shorter plate than the one fitted to a spring tree, as the strain on a spring tree is greater. In some saddles where the stress and strain is greater, like in polo and steeplechase saddles, an extra strip of steel is fitted along the arms of the tree from cantle to head to give an added safety factor; for in the case of a heavy fall, should the wood break, then the steel is more likely to hold and keep the saddle tree in one piece. In the case of flat-race saddles very thin but strong strips of steel are used, and in these saddles and their trees lightness is the key factor; therefore their making is a specialist field and not to be muddled with ordinary saddles about which we are talking now. With spring trees it will be noticed that there are long bands of spring steel running from cantle to head, but not following the line of the tree framework; these are the springs, and if care is not exercised to see that the panel is kept in good condition with sufficient stuffing, they can and will cause undue pressure on the sides of the horse's spine, as can be realized from looking at fig. 27, where the springs can be clearly seen resting on either side of Myth's backbone. Fail to protect the springs adequately, then add the rider's weight on top of them, and one has a perfect recipe for a sore back; the result should not be hard to visualize, especially if the rider is the sort always shifting about in the saddle!

The tree is now complete save for the bars to carry the stirrup leathers. These have to take considerable weight at times and can be either forged or cast, according to the quality of the finished saddle. Forged are always the best and safest, and if one looks at the outside of the bar the word forged should be stamped on it. Returning to figs. 24, 25 and 26, we can see both recessed and ordinary bars. Recessed bars are normally used on spring trees and rigid trees where the saddle requires that the bulk of the stirrup leather is reduced under the rider's leg; they are certainly very much more comfortable. The difference can be seen in fig. 24, where I have put two trees — one spring and the other a tree on which a modern hunting saddle will be built — side by side. The undersides of these bars are shown in figs. 25 and 26 respectively. Nowadays these are the main types of bars on the market, though there are variations, principally caused by the finished quality of the saddle. Another variation of the bar on the rigid tree can be seen in fig. 28, which is a cheaper version and is fixed by only one rivet instead of two in the better-class bar. In days gone by there were many more designs of bars to choose from, but, like bits, the numbers have dwindled over the years, though one still sometimes comes across a crescent-shaped bar that works by means of swinging outwards from one end hooked under a fixed part riveted on to the tree (fig. 29). In general they were to be found on some types of felt saddles and older types of leather saddles. I have seen a fair number myself. If one studies the bars, one will notice a piece hinged up at the end; this is known as the ''thumbpiece'' or safety catch and in the interests of safety should be left open. The idea is that it flies open when one falls off, thereby releasing one's stirrup leather. In fact, very soon they become too stiff to work and are therefore really far safer left open. In the photographs they are in the closed position. In the case of a rigid tree with ordinary bars, the stirrup leather will sometimes shoot off at the wrong moment if there is not sufficient stuffing behind the bars in the panel to hold them on. I have only known this happen once, and that was hunting on Exmoor. The pony I had been lent had rather flat sides and her saddle was old and not overfull of stuffing, though fitting her perfectly satisfactorily; the result was as we galloped up out of a very steep coombe the stirrup leather shot off backwards – much to my discomfort! This was a case where it was necessary to shut the bars (on this saddle they were easily worked) and even so the leathers still came off, but not so frequently; it is not a practice, though, I would advocate. The Exmoor coombes are very steep indeed and present their own problem in saddling; my own mare, Points, a 15 hands 1 inch near thorough-bred, lost her saddle backwards, almost to her loins, once, in the same coombe, though properly girthed up. I had no breast-plate on and she was inclined to run up light out hunting. Recessed bars, on the other hand, if they have a fault, it lies in the fact that they tend to hold the stirrup leathers on rather too tightly in some cases, especially if the stuffing behind the bars is fairly full. In fact when the saddle is on and girthed up it is often impossible to put on the stirrup leather without first undoing the girth. The reason for this is twofold. First, the stirrup bar being recessed is harder to get at; and secondly, the stuffing tends to push the flap out beyond the end of the thumbpiece. It is easily overcome, though, one merely undoes the girth, tips forward the saddle and slips on the leather, before re-girthing. It is done in a minute and normally one puts ones stirrup leathers on first. The alteration of leathers while mounted is quite easy – not hampered at all. Providing one has stirrup irons of the right size to fit one's boot, then I do not think there is any risk from the safety point of view; should one fall and get dragged, then, providing one's stirrup leathers are of the correct size to fit the stirrup bars – neither too thin nor too thick or wide – the leather should come off as easily as with an ordinary-type stirrup bar. The virtues of the recessed bar far outweigh any disadvantages they might seemingly possess – or at least I believe they do. A point, though, that must be remembered is that suppleness of the leather is the governing factor: a well-kept saddle and leathers will ensure the latter's release in the case of a fall – stiff, unkept leather will prevent it!

The shape of the tree determines the future shape of the saddle and its fit. Some horses have very wide backs, while others narrow ones – what will fit one will not fit the other. In the old days this was particularly true; the rigid tree with its long rigid points offered little latitude in fit, especially if it had a straight head. The modern spring tree with its sloping head and flexible points, on the other hand, offers a tolerable degree of latitude, owing to the head being angled away from the withers, thereby reducing the risk of interfering with them, while at the same time bringing the points and bars forward. The flexible points, too, though of no great length, do afford both rider and horse a greater degree of comfort. The rider benefits from having no solid point under his thigh as can happen in old types of saddles with a point of any length; the horse, on the other hand, benefits from the fact that the panel can mould itself to the contours of the shoulder blade and muscles that lie under it, giving more freedom of movement. In order to overcome the many shapes and widths of withers, especially high ones, trees come in many widths and with, in the case of a straight head, also a cut-back head – either a quarter, half or full, as can be seen in figs. 30 and 31; the object of this is to enable the tree to fit easily on either side of the withers, without the risk of interfering with them.

The shape of the seat also varies. Modern all-purpose and jumping saddles have a pronounced dip to their seat, whether they are built on a rigid tree or a spring one. Hunting and riding saddles still tend to have a flatter seat, though not so much as old ones, while dressage saddles, again built on either spring or rigid trees, have a very marked dip to help the rider remain in the correct position. Nevertheless, all modern saddles tend to have a much narrower waist or twist than those of prewar days. This means that at long last the rider's thighs are no longer expected to cope with a wide object that merely prevents them from gripping properly, especially if the rider was short in the leg. In those days, too, the seat was flatter and more often than not inclined towards the rear, throwing the rider's weight on to the cantle and in consequence the loins, and if the panel was not sufficiently stuffed to raise the cantle plate clear of the backbone when the rider was mounted, the pressure was quite considerable. Mercifully only relatively few of these saddles remain – though remain they do; but even the die-hards are beginning to realize that a dip in the seat adds considerable comfort to one's day in the saddle and helps one remain in the correct place.

In order to fit all sizes of horses and ponies – as well as riders – trees have to be made and stocked in a great many sizes and fittings, ranging from the tiny pony to the full size (fig. 32). Anything out of the ordinary, like an exceptionally wide tree (fig. 33), has to be ordered specially. When an order for a saddle comes in the saddler has to go to the store (fig. 32) and select the required tree for the saddle in question. According to the type of saddle, he then has to cut the various parts, using patterns. A hunting saddle will have fairly straight flaps, but not so straight as a show saddle (fig. 34); the difference can be seen in the tiny child's show saddle sitting on top of a full-sized hunting saddle. On the other hand, an all-purpose saddle will have its flaps cut fairly far forward to enable the rider to adopt a shorter leather, while the show-jumping saddle will be cut even further forward still. If the saddle is to have blocked flaps – that is, flaps that fit over a knee roll on the sweat flap like a cap – the flap is damped and tacked over a block of the same size as the knee roll and left to dry; it will then be the shape of the knee roll.

All saddles built on a tree start life the same way. Setting up the seat is an exacting job and can make or mar the finished saddle. It is the whole foundation (fig. 35) and therefore great care has to be expended at this stage. First the saddler fastens the long webs from the head to the cantle; these pre-strained webs are fixed by tiny nails put close together with a narrow piece of leather under their heads to prevent the webs tearing away, for the tingles, as they are called, have very tiny heads and could easily pull through without this precaution; blue tacks are also used. The webs at this stage look like the crosspiece of a bow, standing well clear of the tree underneath it. This is to ensure the seat is really firm and will not sag in later life. Next the strap webs are fitted; we can see these, for they run across the twist of the saddle, over the top of the long webs, and will take the billets or girth straps in due course. At least the rear two billets, for the point strap is fitted later and in most cases does not go right over the tree – though I believe some saddlers now put the point strap right over in front of the strap webs. Behind the strap web comes the back web, with the back straining canvas – in cheap saddles hessian is used in place of canvas – the latter two are stitched together. The webs that traverse the tree and long webs force the latter down tight to make a firm, springy base for the rest of the saddle seat. Now the bellies (fig. 36) are fitted to prevent the seat of the saddle falling away under the rider's weight, leaving him to sit on the hard tree – these are small pre-shaped pieces of leather. One can easily realize that it is essential to have the tree made out of a material that will accept nails and in which they can grip, for many nails and tacks are used in the making of a saddle!

In the case of a tree with flexible points – which are made out of leather, hence the reason why they can mould themselves to the outline of the horse's shoulder – the points are now riveted on to the blunt ends of the head and then bound with either linen tape or thin leather, to prevent any rough edges. Where the tree has also springs, then these, too, are bound with either linen tape or thin leather (firms vary in their methods slightly), to prevent rusting and, should the stuffing in the panel slip, the horse from getting injured – for, as I explained earlier, this could happen. It is interesting to study fig. 37, for, as one can see, the tape-covered springs and the flexible points are very clear, and also the long webs as they run from the head to cross over at the twist and fasten to the cantle. The trees in the background show the points from the front. The springs must always be spaced far enough apart to allow ample room for the clearance of the horse's spine – otherwise, especially with a thin horse, untold damage could result.

All firms do not make their saddles quite the same way, but basically the variation is not all that great. Some saddlers use linen thread; others are now using nylon, as it is stronger and lasts longer, even if it does not look so nice. No doubt one gets used to it and if it cuts down repair bills then it is worth it. The making of panels, too, varies from firm to firm, as will be seen, which means the order of make-up has to vary, too.

The seat is now ready for its cover and padding. Wool was used in the old days and still is in some saddles, but plastic foam and foam rubber have found their place in the saddlery trade in this modern age. In the old days the seats were set – that is, serge was drawn over the tree and wool set into the seat through a small slit in the centre of the top by means of a long pliable rod, known as a seat steel (fig. 38), and then shifted into place by means of an awl (fig. 39), which is poked through the serge (panels are regulated the same way with a slightly longer awl) when and where it is wanted to even out the wool. This completed, the slit is neatly sewn up. In cheap saddles the wool was put directly on to the tree and then hessian on top of that. Nowadays it is the growing practice to use plastic foam, which is cut out and shaped to fit – the plastic foam can be seen in the forefront of fig. 40 – these are, in fact, panels, but the foam is the same, and it makes a very comfortable foundation to the seat. In the case of the foam seats, best-quality linen is stretched over the webs and nailed down neatly (fig. 41) and then the plastic foam is fitted on top of it (fig. 42). The tree is now ready for the seat covering – in this case pigskin. The unblocked seat can be seen in fig. 41, beyond the tree, along with the other parts. The seat is now blocked – that is, damped and nailed on to the tree and left to dry – by which time it is blocked to the shape of the tree. The skirts are tacked on next and trimmed to fit. Both are then removed and sewn together with a hide welt. In cheaper saddles the backs are then machined on, but in expensive ones they are sewn on by hand, the object of the backs being to enable the seat to be nailed to the tree. A seat ready for fitting can be seen in fig. 43, which shows it from the underside. It is not surprising that saddles are expensive when one sees how much hand work goes into them – from first to last. Fitting the seat is an exacting job requiring skill and strong fingers (fig. 44), and once safely nailed on it has to be trimmed (fig. 45). On the right-hand side of these two photographs a pile of seats (the correct way up) can be seen waiting to be fitted. Though this particular firm uses principally plastic foam for its seats, sorbo, sponge or foam rubber is used extensively by many firms both in England and on the Continent, and probably throughout the world, though the greater majority of saddles are made in Europe. It is a matter of choice.

The girth straps are fitted next. First the two that go on to the strap web are sewn firmly on to the web that has been doubled up for extra strength – our safety depends on these straps; in saddles that have only two girth straps, then only one strap is sewn on to this web – should the saddle have a point web right over the tree then the point strap is sewn on, otherwise it is fitted after the flaps. Either vegetable or chrome straps can be used; in fig. 46 we have a saddle with chrome straps – these are strong and long lasting. It is an interesting photograph, as it illustrates clearly just how the springs lie – the offside one is very noticeable; so, too, are the flexible points and the rivets that hold on the gullet plate. Along the far edge and inside the head the nails fixing the seat can be seen. I have just mentioned the point strap, the girth strap lying next to the horse's elbow; in reality, when horsemen talk of a point strap they are not referring to this strap, but to another one which is nailed on to the outside of the point of the tree itself (fig. 47), the object being to help keep the saddle back – it is found principally on show saddles and children's saddles.

The saddle is now ready to have its flaps fitted. Should the flap have inset knee grips of doeskin (or buckskin) inlaid with sponge rubber or plastic foam, then these are fitted first – many jumping and eventing saddles have them to enable the rider to grip better (fig. 48). Having fitted the saddle flap of the required shape and the point strap, the sweat flap follows in the case of the modern foam Saumur panels, care being exercised to ensure that both flaps are even (fig. 49), as failure to do this would result in the whole saddle being thrown out of alignment. On the floor some rigid trees are waiting their turn and it is interesting to note that all the work of assembly is done on benches covered with a pad of something soft to prevent damage to the saddles – leather scratches very easily. Knee rolls are not fitted to all saddles, but should they be required they are sewn on before the flap is fitted in the case of these foam Saumur panels (fig. 50), as they are attached to the outside of these flaps to come beneath the saddle flap. The flaps in place, then the gullet lining and forepiece – a welt that goes round the front arch of the head of the tree inside the pommel – are added in their turn. The gullet lining can be seen in fig. 51, where the panel (leather-covered plastic foam Saumur) is, in fact, being fitted over its edge. The fittings such as staples, ''D's'' and rivets, often bearing the name of the saddler who made the saddle, are fitted next in their respective places. These rivets can be seen in fig. 52 in the two saddles nearest the camera, which are awaiting their panels – one through the skirt and the other through the flap; in the old days there used to be two more, one on either side of the seat through the tail end of the skirt, and they are still to be seen on the Count Toptani and the French and Italian saddles (figs. 81, 88 and 86). The object of these nails or rivets is to hold the skirt and saddle flaps securely on to the tree.

The saddle is now complete save for its panel. These panels vary considerably and fall into three principal groups. Those stuffed with wool; those employing felt, plastic foam, sponge rubber or foam rubber, and lastly those which fall outside either of these two categories, and into this section I have put the sorbo rubber panels used in some side-saddles and the pneumatic panels. There also used to be a panel called a Wykeham panel made out of shaped pieces of felt that could be removed from the tree, so adjusting its fit. I have only seen one once and that was at Porlockford in 1954; when I was there we were shown it, but it was never used. Like all things, panels come and go; the best survive and go on being used, while others die a natural death through impracticability.

The stuffed panels – using a special wool, white for super saddles and grey for ordinary ones, resilient to weight and disinclined to go lumpy (an important factor, for a lumpy panel can cause a sore back) – embrace six different kinds of panels, namely Continental, Saumur, All-in-One, Full Panel, Half Panel and Short Panel, while the second group covers the Saumur and Rugby panels using the materials mentioned in group two. Both used felt, but now plastic foam and sponge and foam rubber are proving popular.

The procedure for fitting only differs slightly with both groups. Taking the modern Saumur and Rugby panels first – the plastic foam is cut to shape and covered in leather. In fig. 53 the saddler takes his prepared panel from the top of a pile of plastic foam to begin. Note the point of the tree is on the underside of the sweat flap and not on the outside as with ordinary saddles. The point-strap web can also be seen nailed on next to the point of the tree behind the stirrup bar. Next he starts to lace in the panel (fig. 54). The point pocket in the back of the panel, which in this type of panel will be out of sight when finished, can be seen directly beneath his right hand. Figs. 55 and 56 show the lacing in progress – this must be done very carefully or the finished appearance will be spoilt and the panel crooked. Fig. 57 gives another stage in securing the panel, while fig. 58 is a job well done — the completed saddle after a final apprizal is about to be placed on the saddle horse on top of a pile of basil, which in due course will be used to back stuffed panels. In the case of true Rugby panels (figs. 47 and 59), the felt to fill them is cut to shape and covered in leather, before being laced in in more or less the same manner. Under the girth straps the free sweat flap can be seen, this flap is also a form of girth safe and its job in life is to prevent the girth buckles from sticking into the horse. These panels are found a lot on show saddles, as they afford a very close contact with the horse; sometimes they are also known as Whippy panels after the famous firm who made so many.

    In the case of stuffed panels, the panels are cut out first and then sewn together with their welting — in leather-lined saddles the gullet is left open, but in serge ones the panel is closed, that is filled in with serge across the gullet — and the point pocket of hide is stitched in place; the backing of these panels is often of basil. The panel is then stuffed with either white or grey wool according to its finished quality, which is passed into the panel through small slits in the back, which can just be seen if one looks closely at fig. 60 (in the background of which is the seat in figs. 44 and 45, now nearing completion). A wisp of wool is, in fact, visible protruding from the front slit on the nearside panel (on top of the bench). This is a short panel. The same type of panel can be seen on two separate saddles in fig. 61, which gives the underside of the panel (a serge-lined Barnsby Pony Club saddle), and fig. 62, showing the panel as it lies beneath the saddle flap (this is an ordinary riding saddle, also serge lined). In common with the half panel, which is an inch or so longer than the short panel, but only reaches half-way down the flap, and the full panel (figs. 63 and 64), in which we have a serge-lined steeplechase saddle with "Tod Sloan" flap, cut extra far forward to let the rider use a very short leather (note the loose sweat flap under the girth straps to protect the basil on the back of the panel — this loose flap is found on all these sort of panels and Rugby panels), it has been quilted and the backing (the bit showing) cross barred. Continental panels (figs. 65 and 66) give us an English saddle with a panel I personally like a great deal. In the former photograph we can see how the panel is cut all in one piece on each side, so doing away with any joins to rub the horse, and in the latter one the knee rolls, with their extra roll on top and the thigh rolls, separated by the sweat flap, which is a flat piece of hide stitched down, thereby eliminating all unnecessary bulk under one's legs. Figs. 67 and 68 represent an Italian-made saddle, of similar construction to the first, but with an additional sweat flap under the girth straps and a reinforcement along the bottom of the panel. We next have a saddle built on the lines of a Saumur, but with a thigh roll. In fact, it is a classical dressage saddle built in England with an extra long girth strap and using a special short girth (figs. 69 and 70). Glanced at quickly it closely resembles a Continental panel, but in truth the sweat flap is only one thickness of hide and not part of the panel itself, being sewn on to the panel and the thigh rolls being let into the sweat flap from the underside, whereas with a true Continental panel like those in figs. 65, 66, 67 and 68 which we have just seen the thigh and knee rolls are merely sandwiched down by the sweat flap in between them — they are part and parcel of the panel. We now come to the true Saumur panel, called after the famous French Equitation School at Saumur and sometimes known as a French panel. This panel (figs. 71 and 72) has the sweat flap sewn on to the panel and no thigh roll. Many variations are to be found; one is seen in figs. 73

and 74, where a short thigh roll has been inserted at the top of the flap; whereas they can also have a block on the back of the sweat flap in place of a thigh roll. One English firm on their show-jumping saddle uses this and so does the French firm in their show-jumping saddle (fig. 75); in this saddle the panel more closely resembles the modern plastic foam Saumur panel, as it is stuffed with foam rubber and not wool. It belongs therefore in group two, but unlike the plastic foam panels the point of the tree is on the outside of the sweat flap. The newest of the stuffed panels is the All-in-One (fig. 76). The skirt and saddle flap are cut in one piece and so, too, is the panel lining of leather; these two are then sewn together with an inlay of foam rubber for softness; the girth straps, on extra long webs (they are stitched on just inside the panel opening), come out of a hole at the bottom of the panel. The foam is visible if one looks closely at the girth straps where they emerge from the panel; it is just behind them. On some saddles where it is required to raise the seat at the back a gusset is let into the panel so that more stuffing can be inserted in this region, so giving a bearing surface along the whole panel. Though no doubt different people have different names for it, it is generally known as a Melbourne facing or German panel, and can be seen on the following saddles – figs. 84, 90 and 93. It is very useful in a dressage saddle with a short seat, as it means that the rider's weight is distributed over as wide an area as possible. The method of lacing in these panels is similar to those we saw being put in earlier – the two do not differ much.

The lining of a saddle is a matter of choice, and can be either leather, linen, serge, silk or nylon, the last two being used for flat-race saddles where lightness is the keynote. Leather is undoubtedly the best – the most expensive to buy – but if well cared for, kept clean and soft and not allowed to become hard and caked with dried sweat, will last a very long time indeed. It is easy to keep clean, if done each time it is used, and retains its shape, thereby reducing its maintenance costs and – here is a point – unnecessary veterinary bills! This last because, providing it has its yearly overhaul and check to see that all is well, it will be less likely to cause a sore back than some of the others and, too, should there be any skin infection around, then a leather lining can be much more easily disinfected than any of the other sorts – a wipe with a piece of cloth wrung out in diluted Savlon willl take care of it. Linen (used always over serge) is good – cool in summer and fairly easy to keep clean by wiping and scrubbing at intervals; it also keeps its shape fairly well and when worn can be replaced by one's own saddler (figs. 77 and 78). The linen must be fitted carefully and stretched on tightly over the serge panel, which has been regulated first, care being exercised to see that no wrinkles or creases have been left, as these would rub and trouble result in time. An old saddle, the rivet referred to earlier can be seen under the saddler's right-hand middle finger. We now come to the lining most commonly found in cheap saddles – serge. It has many disadvantages and some advantages. Being a fine white woollen material, it has a lot of give in it, resulting in it causing the panel to lose its shape very quickly. Unless care is taken to have the panel regulated as soon as this happens, before long the gullet will be found to be closed, leaving no channel along the horse's spine. Its maintenance costs are high, for unlike leather that, once regulated a few months after purchase (all stuffed panels, regardless of their linings, sink when first used and have to have more stuffing added to fill them up to the required amount), it does not retain this satisfactory state for long and needs frequent regulating to maintain a usable condition. Not only do they go lumpy, but the stuffing shifts often leaving the edges of the tree and cantle unprotected and the head resting far too close to the withers. For this reason these saddles need a lot of watching it they are not to cause sore backs. You can clean them by brushing with a stiff brush when dry to remove all traces of mud and dried sweat, which will not only rot the panel but also rub the horse, especially a thin-skinned one, and when very dirty scrubbing them, though they take a long time to dry. So often one sees a serge-lined saddle with great holes in the underside of the panel just where the weight of the rider brings it in contact with the horse's back. The owner no doubt is too ignorant to realize the risk he is running of a sore back or too callous to care and just pinch penny, grudging the money required to have the saddle relined. This is quite expensive and another thing against serge as a lining that is going to get a lot of hard use. In its favour, though, it has one thing the other linings do not have – the ability to enable the saddler to regulate the stuffing by merely sticking a panel awl (fig. 79)* through the material where he wants to, and then shifting the stuffing around to the correct place to fit the horse's back. With a difficult back to fit this is a great advantage; in this case, providing they are kept fully stuffed and beaten at regular intervals – yes, I mean this – they are satisfactory. The object of beating the panel with one's riding cane is to break down the lumps so that the stuffing retains its resilience. Serge also has the added advantage of being warm. Some horses dislike the feel of something cold and clammy on their backs, though they will accept it once warm, while others, though accepting the saddle when cool, will object once it gets hot and clammy, as leather can. For these customers, serge is a blessing, for unless a numnah is used under the saddle they will spend their time trying to down both rider and saddle, and nothing is more tiresome or uncomfortable – both for horse and rider alike, and who can blame the horse, not the rider! The other two linings, silk and nylon, are used in flat-race saddles, as they reduce the weight. So much for the different kinds of saddle linings; they each have their merits and their disadvantages; the choice really is governed by one's horse, one's purse and one's own personal preference.

We now come to the third group of panels in which I have placed the rubber panels (that is, the pink, and sometimes grey, sorbo rubber that is used for the panel of a side-saddle – these are very thick and not covered like the other panels we have discussed) and also the pneumatic panels. These are, I believe, made both in this country and also in Germany, but are not, anyway in this country, in general use.

Before turning to the saddles themselves, a word about the shape of the cantle; these can be either square or round, as will be seen if we study the various photographs of the saddles and trees. The former is found largely on rigid trees, while the latter is favoured for spring trees, though it is found on rigid ones, too. In the case of the spring tree it has the advantage that the rider has no natural finger grip as he has with the square one, and therefore must put his hand right over and grip the saddle flap when mounting – essential if the tree of a spring-tree saddle is not to be twisted out of alignment, which can happen owing to its flexibility. In the case of a rigid tree, it is a matter of personal preference – the tree itself is the same.

* Top row, second from right.

Part Two – Saddles

Turning now to the saddles themselves – we have a variety of types to choose from according to the branch of equestrian sport or equitation we wish to partake in, for the more specialized branches require their own type of saddle. Nevertheless, each firm makes its own variations of a given type of saddle, employing slight modifications to achieve this; but in principle each type or group of saddles more or less conform to a given pattern – some being better in design than others – just the same way as bits varied within their respective groups. Unlike bits, though, though group names such as show jumping, hunting, general purpose and show, etc., all denote a given type of saddle, a trade name like Beaufort (Eldonian), Burghley (Eldonian), Xenophon (Gibson), Holberg (Gibson), Fulmer (Turf and Travel) and Invicta (Turf and Travel), to mention only a few at random, does not mean that another firm using the same name will necessarily make a saddle of the same type. For this reason one must always state the name of the firm if one requires a given type of saddle, as well as its trade name – otherwise, unwittingly you could land yourself with a show saddle, say, when you, in fact, wanted a cross-country saddle. I do not say it would happen, but it quite easily could if the name was not a registered one. The one exception is really the Lane Fox, for this is not a trade name but a type – many firms make Lane Fox saddles, American walking horse show saddles, giving them their own trade names as well. One good example of the same name being given to two differently constructed saddles comes in the "Featherweight" show-jumping saddles. The one made by Crosby and Co. Ltd., of the Olympic Works, Walsall, is, to look at, a conventionally built saddle with a skirt and saddle flap separate and a panel with short girth straps, whereas, on the other hand, the "Featherweight" show-jumping saddle from the "Cliff-Barnsby" stable of Jabez Cliff and Co. Ltd., of the Globe Works, Walsall, is constructed with an all-in-one panel with a Melbourne facing and long girth straps – both of their type, equally good – but of totally different design, which goes to illustrate how essential it is to mention the firm's name as well as that of the saddle and its type when ordering from a saddler who may stock more than one firm's saddles. It is wise too, to state the type of panel required, for some saddles can be made with more than one type, besides linings. In this way you can avoid landing yourself with a saddle far removed from anything you had visualized!

Great Britain is renowned for its saddles, which are exported to all corners of the Globe; even so, other countries make some excellent saddles, too – Italy, France and Germany in particular. We, in fact, have learnt a lot from them, and no doubt they from us – both in the past and probably in the future, too. With the advent of the forward seat – the balanced seat as generally adopted in this country is a moderated form – it was, as I said earlier, necessary to build a saddle which would allow the rider to position his body over the centre of gravity and maintain it there at all times, without, as happened with the old type of saddle and those built with forward flaps using the old design of tree, sliding to the rear behind the movement. To achieve this the saddle, whether sprung seat or rigid, must have a pronounced dip which enables the rider to sit in the centre of the saddle at its lowest point nearest the horse's back and a panel so constructed as to afford the maximum support, comfort and security to the rider by assisting him to fix his knees and thighs in the correct position and reducing the bulk under them by means of a narrow twist and recessed bars, together with the angled head and thin sweat flap – regardless of the length of leather adopted by the rider.

The change in this country was slow coming – the First World War came and went before we saw any real advance – then, thanks largely to the farsightedness of one man with a good knowledge of horses himself, aided by three extremely able and experienced horsemen, the change came about. To Lieut.-Colonel F. E. Gibson this country – in fact, the whole riding world – owes a genuine debt of gratitude, for it was he who gave us our modern saddles as we know them today. The transition from the old type to the new is an interesting one. Between the wars the late Lieut.-Colonel Hance, while running his famous school at Malvern, complained to his one-time pupil of St. John's Wood days – Colonel Gibson – that he could not teach his pupils satisfactorily if they were forced to sit on their horse's loins. Aided by an old broken-treed Australian saddle, possessed of a considerable dip to its seat, Colonel Hance and Colonel Gibson evolved the Distas Central Position saddle – called after Colonel Gibson's saddlery firm – a saddle that evoked considerable laughter when first seen at Olympia just prior to the war. But for the war intervening we might well have had our modern saddles ten years sooner than we eventually received them. In the pre-1939 era Continental saddlers, too, were beginning to build saddles that encouraged and enabled the rider to adopt the forward seat; in this country the majority of our saddles still lacked a dip to their seats, though Owen's saddles were an exception, for this firm did make their saddles with a reasonable dip to the seat. The war over, Colonel Gibson * joined forces with Count Ilias Toptani to produce the Toptani show-jumping saddle – the saddle that was to influence all other jumping saddles, including those made by Pariani of Italy, besides being the forerunner of all the all-purpose and general-purpose saddles that we have today. About this time, away down on Exmoor, another very gifted horseman was engaged in running his successful riding school at Porlock – the late Captain Tony Collings, who in 1950 had ridden the winner of the Three Day Event at Badminton, Miss G. H. Crystal's Remus, and was to train the British Three Day Event Team for the 1952 Olympics. A pupil himself of Colonel Hance, it was he who discovered the trainer of our Gold Medal Three Day Event Olympic team of 1968, Mr Bertie Hill, who himself had been a member of that 1952 team and in the Gold Medal team of 1956 and again in the 1960 team. Realizing the need for a saddle that would embrace all three phases of eventing besides just jumping, and also be suitable for such sports as polo and hunting – not to mention hacking and all the many other activities the ordinary rider partakes in either for sport or pleasure – Captain Collings approached Colonel Gibson, who had his firm at Great Gransden in Bedfordshire (before moving in 1957 to Newmarket – F. E. Gibson (Saddlers) Ltd., of Sales Paddock Lane), and between them they adapted post war saddles to produce the now world-famous "Gibson All-Purpose" saddle (fig. 80) – the original of all the many many varieties of general and all-purpose saddles now on the market. A wonderful saddle, embracing all the very necessary

---

* Colonel Gibson on returning from the war represented Messrs. George Parker's 'outside' from 1946 to December 1953. In this time the original Toptani and the original All Purpose were developed and sold from this firm, and thereafter the All Purpose from Colonel Gibson's own firm.

features of a really good modern saddle, it was first launched in 1952 and has since then stood the test of time. By now some of the other really good saddles – and there are some extremely good ones on the market today, besides some that certainly do not match up to the standard required for such a saddle – may well have equalled the "Gibson All-Purpose" saddle, but I doubt, even so, if it has really been surpassed; which is why I have chosen it to illustrate the modern saddle in all the feature photographs – and, too, it is the original.

Taking the first group of saddles that employ a full tree. Whereas the greater majority of modern saddles are now built on a spring tree, a considerable number are still built on a rigid tree of modern design, the main difference between the two being in the springs; for both types of trees go in for a sloping head – though it is more common to the spring tree (fig. 24), and I only found it in the rigid trees with the Pony Club one. Against that, all spring trees do not have a sloping head; fig. 27 shows us one with a cut-back head on a dressage tree.

The finish of a saddle varies, too – some have plain leather flaps and skirts, either hide or pigskin-covered hide, while others have reversed hide. This is found in racing – flat and steeplechasing – and show and hunting saddles. And now we have brushed pigskin (which is the grain side of pigskin brushed), as, too, what is known as velvet hide (the grain side of butt leather brushed to make it look like suede or doeskin), which in its own right is used not only for covering knee grips on the flaps but also the seats and skirts, too, and the whole flap.

English and Continental show-jumping saddles are made very akin to one another – as, too, are most saddles made in Europe, regardless of the side of the Channel. Probably the best-known jumping saddle is that made by George Parker of London – the Count Toptani (fig. 81). Strictly speaking, a jumping saddle is constructed longer in the seat and has its flaps set further forward than a general or all-purpose saddle, owing to the fact that the rider uses a shorter leather for top-class show jumping than the rider using a general-purpose saddle who needs to adjust his leathers to suit his form of riding at the time. I have noticed, though, that many saddlers are recommending their jumping saddles for general-purpose saddles or for cross-crountry work. In the case of the Count Toptani the saddle has more than one style of flap, so the rider must make sure which flap he is buying if he wants the saddle for a specific branch of equitation. Figs. 82, 83 and 84 are all designed for show jumping and built on spring trees, but of different construction, fig. 84 being made with a skirt and flap cut in one and an all-in-one panel, as seen in fig. 76. The Italian firm of Pariani of Milan not only has its very good conventional jumping saddles (figs. 85 and 86) but also does one that dispenses with a flap and uses a special short girth to reduce bulk under the rider's leg (fig. 87), while from France the old-established firm of Hermes of Paris gives us a saddle, though principally a jumping saddle (fig. 88), that can be used as a general-purpose one, too.

We come to the general-purpose saddles next and start with one that runs the "Gibson All-Purpose" very close, for it is a very good saddle (fig. 89), and for the rider who is long in the leg an excellent one, for it has a specially long distance from cantle to swell of the knee so as to let the rider's knee rest in the correct place behind the knee roll. We now have two rigid tree saddles of the general-purpose group (figs. 90 and 91), while fig. 92 gives us a modern hunting saddle also on a rigid tree. This latter one is a very good example of what a hunting saddle should look like; it is not very far removed from the rigid-tree type of general-purpose saddles. Unlike its forebears – hunting saddles more often than not sloped towards the rear – it is well balanced and has a very definite dip to its seat, thereby enabling the rider to sit centrally without the risk of his weight – very often considerable – resting on the cantle and its accompanying steel plates.

Dressage saddles come next. Since the war advanced dressage has become very much more popular in this country and with it the need for a saddle specially designed for this form of riding. Though the main principles of tree design of modern saddles remains regarding the deep seat and narrow twist, some features have had to be altered to conform with the different style of riding. The seat of a dressage saddle is much shorter, so as to keep the rider in a central position, and varies from 16 to 17 inches according to the firm – 16 to $16\frac{1}{2}$ inches being the more accepted length. The head of the tree does not slope as in a jumping saddle, but is straight, either with or without a cut-back head, and bars that extend to the rear so as to let the leather hang down the centre of the flap. The flap in its turn is far straighter, though the panel remains similar and is normally of Continental type. Some, though not all, dressage saddles have only two girth straps and these, instead of being short, are attached to long webs and employ a short girth – so as to remove the buckles from under the rider's leg. Owing to the very short seat it is essential to ensure the saddle is well stuffed in the panel under the rider; for this a Melbourne facing is often required, though not all dressage saddles have it. They vary considerably according to the firm who makes them. In the old days they were adaptations of show saddles and the cut-back Owen type of saddle with a semi-Continental style of panel. The principal change in this country resulted through another example of collaboration between a firm of saddlers with definite horse knowledge and an experienced rider. In this case it was Turf and Travel Ltd., of Gerrards Cross, and Mr. Robert Hall, who taught the classical dressage seat of the Spanish School at his own school at Fulmer a few miles away. The result was the now famous Fulmer dressage saddle (fig. 93) – very much a purpose-built saddle and not one to be used for other branches of riding that require the rider to use a shorter leather. The other dressage saddle is an example of another design (fig. 94), having a half-cut-back head and short girth straps. Though the Fulmer is built on a rigid tree, some dressage saddles are built on spring trees (fig. 27) – like jumping and general-purpose saddles – each firm has its own designs and styles within a given principle of design.

Show saddles follow. These are designed to show off the horse's conformation and especially his front – not for the comfort of the rider! Some are far more exaggerated than others, having their flaps cut back behind the vertical, leaving the rider no room for his knees at all; these, in fact, look anything but nice and can be very ugly, from my own personal way of thinking. Very popular in hack and show pony classes, they are not so often seen in hunter classes, where the trend is to use a saddle with a little more flap to balance the picture and help the rider. I often think judges would prefer a more reasonable type of saddle with something to sit on; for after all they have to ride many different horses in the course of a day's judging, and a good, comfortable saddle must make their ride that bit more pleasant – and the ride counts for a lot! Fig. 95 is not too exaggerated and shows us the close-fitting panel necessary for a show saddle – Rugby or short panels are usual in this type of saddle – but whichever type of panel it must be of sufficient thickness and resilience to ensure adequate protection for the horse's back and clearance for its withers, once the rider is mounted. As most show horses are shown in big condition, this is not the problem that it would be if they were on the lean side, when the risk of pressure on the spine and withers would be very definite with this type of thin panel. In this case the quarter-cut-back head allows a certain amount of clearance of the withers and the seat is of sufficient depth to help the rider sit centrally rather than on the cantle, as does happen with the straighter type of seat. The Lane Fox family of show saddles is particularly bad in this respect. Some are fairly reasonable (fig. 96), but many have very flat seats that force the rider to sit right back – in fact their whole make-up is designed with this aim in view. Long seats – 19–22 inches – very straight flaps often behind the vertical and so wide as to come almost back to the cantle, are the main features of this family, together with a full-cut-back head; as can be imagined, the rider's whole weight is placed so far back as to come either on or over the loins in a great many cases. It is a saddle that belongs to the American market for their special type of show classes; but it is sold as a show saddle in this country, and to my mind is unsuitable as such, as our horses are of a different stamp to theirs, which are much bigger and stronger than our own show hacks. In this country we often place our normal show saddles far enough back, as it is, to show off our horse's shoulder and front, employing a point strap to achieve this, without using an extra-long-seated saddle into the bargain. The true show saddle is strictly a specialist saddle meant only for the show ring and not for everyday riding and jumping as one sometimes sees it used – especially by children. Before long we may very well see an adaptation of the modern dressage saddle for use in the show ring – one thing very often leads to another, as we have seen already – it only really needs one well-known figure in any given field to bring about the change!

Children's saddles are normally scaled-down models of full-sized saddles (fig. 97) with some slight modifications to make them less expensive, though except in the case of what are termed school saddles (figs. 98 and 99), which are medium-priced saddles designed for use in riding schools and for teaching the young without costing a fortune – they actually come in all sizes and cater for grown-ups, too – the tendency is now to make children's saddles of much better quality, and above all design, even if they cost more. Fig. 100 is an example of this; a well-designed saddle for the very small, it has only a 12-inch seat, but, and here it is sensible, it has a second pair of flaps that can be fitted when the child has outgrown the first. Its Rugby panel (fig. 47) has extra thickness in the back to raise the seat and prevent it from tipping backwards – a common fault with so many children's saddles, leaving them sitting on a slope – and a deep seat that helps the tiny child of three to ten years get sufficient support and a far better start in its riding than many of the older-type saddles that are far too wide in the twist, forcing the child's thighs apart, thereby removing its grip. Expensive yes, compared with the average child's saddle – though no more than the better-designed saddles for older children – I think it could well be an investment providing care is taken to look after it! Designed as a leading rein saddle and a first child's pony saddle, it can be used in these classes in the show ring as well as for ordinary riding at home – and how much better to put a tiny child on a saddle that will give it some real support and not strain its back, besides making it feel very much more secure. For older children, many of the better-known all-purpose and general-purpose saddles are made in children's sizes, too, so if a parent is prepared to pay for a good, well-designed saddle that will give the child the necessary support and help, then the choice and opportunity is there now. What it really amounts to is, if your child is really good enough and shows enough promise and keenness to warrant it, and above all you can afford to spend the extra money – unfortunately many parents just cannot afford it, however good and promising their child may be – then try to invest in such a saddle, and having done so see to it that the child, regardless of its age, treats it with respect and does not neglect it or leave it lying around to get damaged; good saddles cost a lot of money and therefore should be valued. As for the child whose parents cannot afford a really expensive saddle – well, there is no need to despair; they got there in the old days and they will get there now if they are good enough, and, too, thanks to the Pony Club, we now have the Pony Club Approved saddle, a saddle designed to encourage young riders to ride correctly and get the best out of themselves and their ponies without running their parents straight into the bankruptcy court. First put on the market in 1961, it has gone a long way to improve the general riding in the Pony Club, as can be seen from the standard now reached in the Championships. In 1963 a better slightly more expensive version with a Continental-type panel and more forward flaps was also approved and allowed to be produced by those firms already holding permission to produce the Pony Club Approved saddle. Figs. 101 and 102 show two of the standard type of approved saddle, both with serge panels, but leather ones are available, too, at slightly extra cost. Built to strict specifications of the Pony Club, every saddle is stamped to show it and so, too, is the tree (fig. 103), which is a rigid one with rigid points, but a slightly sloping head and narrow twist. The twist is, in fact, only $5\frac{1}{4}$ inches (as close as I could measure) against 6 inches found in both a small pony tree and the school tree – the spring tree of a jumping saddle being $5\frac{1}{2}$ inches (but more about trees and their fitting in a later chapter), which proves how much better this saddle is than the average saddle bought for children. Too, the seat is fairly deep with a good dip to position the child and maintain him there with comfort. If every child in the Pony Club used an approved saddle, how much more comfortable they would be and how quickly their riding would improve – besides making the instructor's job infinitely more easy, for trying to teach a child to sit correctly when it is slipping off the back of the saddle is as impossible for the instructor as it is for the child. Even if a parent cannot afford a new saddle, there should now be sufficient second-hand ones around to give these other children a chance to own a reasonable saddle that will help rather than hinder their riding. If parents have only a given amount they can afford to spend on their child's new pony, and that child has passed the tiny fat pony stage – in other words is eight or over – and they have not already got a good saddle, then they would be wise to consider giving slightly less for the pony itself and putting the difference – say £10 to £20 – into a good, well-designed saddle that will ensure that both the child and pony are comfortable and happy, and therefore a great deal safer. It is no good trying to save on buying a child's saddle on the cheap; a good saddle is an investment and, providing it has been well cared for, can be exchanged for another good saddle when the child has outgrown it. Once you have got a good saddle you have the means of always having one; it is the initial purchasing that is the problem!

Next on the list of full tree saddles come the Polo saddle (fig. 104). A fast-galloping game, it requires a saddle that will enable the rider to maintain a firm, strong seat; to look at it is not unlike a hunting saddle, but has a very much more pronounced dip to its seat, which is also slightly shorter and wider, and the twist is narrow to allow the rider maximum grip and flexibility of his body when playing at speed. The panel is usually of the Rugby or short type, but sometimes has knee rolls for added support, in which case the panel would be of the Saumur or Continental type. The tree itself is heavily rein-forced at the gullet for added strength, and often has a quarter- or half-cut-back head.

The side-saddle is now not seen so much as it was in the past, though it is still used for ladies' classes – hack and hunter – in the show ring and by some horsewomen in the hunting field, who prefer a side-saddle (fig. 105). In between the wars horsewomen also rode their point-to-points side-saddle, not that many could do it now, and they are far better not trying, for many sit on a side-saddle and bump along, but few horsewomen today really ride side-saddle, which is why their horses get sore backs, not from the fact necessarily that they are carrying a side-saddle. Well done, it can look extremely elegant, and I must say I enjoyed the little I have done. It would be a pity if it dies out altogether – die out, though, it will, unless the tree makers can make the side-saddle tree by modern methods, for at present it is extremely hard to find anyone capable of making a tree (fig. 106), and the firms that specialized in making these saddles have now gone and their saddlers in most cases retired from the trade, though there are still one or two around. Side-saddles normally have a stuffed panel, linen covered or a sorbo rubber one, which is pink in colour, and not covered; these drew the backs rather, though gripped better. Heavy things, side-saddles weigh around 30 lb. for a hunting one against 9–11 lb. for a modern astride saddle, which means, especially if the rider is heavy, the horses are carrying a lot of weight for many hours at a stretch – which is why for hunting I would like to see them go.

Another specialized branch of the saddlery trade is that of making flat-race saddles and to some extent steeplechasing saddles. The former are extremely light and weigh a matter of ounces rather than pounds and the firms who make them are to be found around Newmarket and similar racing centres. Flat-race saddles (fig. 107) are made with very forward flaps and out of very light leather – pigskin is used throughout for flaps as well as for the seat. These saddles, too – that is those under 6 lb. – dispense with the stirrup bars and have in their place a slot which allows the web or leather to be looped round the tree itself. The trees used in these light saddles are also very fragile and can be broken in a man's hand. The panels are full ones (fig. 107 has no panel, having come in for repair!) and lined in either cloth, silk or nylon. Australian saddles, some extremely tiny, have panels of the Saumur type in miniature and are lined, as some now in this country, with thin leather. The reason for this is the fact that leather does not mop up the sweat, whereas cloth will, thereby increasing the all-important factor, weight. The lighter type do not really fit the horse's back in the accepted sense, so have to have a wither pad, a small soft pad that goes between the horse's withers and the head of the saddle.* Owing to their lightness these saddles should not be used for anything other than racing itself, as they fit far too close to the horse's back should a jockey sit on them for long; while racing he is perched up over his saddle and merely requires it to hang his leathers on. The middle-weight saddles range from 6 to 17 lb., and anything over that, up to 30 lb. in some cases, are weighted. Steeplechasing saddles (fig. 108) are much more like an ordinary saddle and made by very many more firms; they come in all weights according to the weight of the rider and that laid down for the race. The over 6 lb. flat-race saddles are made on similar lines, having two girth straps instead of one and proper bars, but both saddles have a light-weight surcingle that goes right over the saddle and lies over the girth; they should pass through the loop on the saddle flap. Both these saddles have what is known as a Tod Sloan flap, but this is not always so — there are other patterns. While, as I said, the flat-race saddle should never be used for anything but racing, the steeplechase saddle can be used and was for jumping in the past, but it is not so good as a general-purpose or proper jumping saddle, as it has not the support of the dipped seat they have. There is also what is known as a race exercise saddle; this is a heavier saddle of about 9 lb. when complete with leathers, irons and girths — a stronger saddle, it is designed to withstand the rigours of everyday use in a busy training stable.

We come now to the second group of saddles — those built on a half tree or head. These saddles are far cheaper and cover both the leather race exercise pad like that in fig. 109, which is growing in popularity, as I now see it in many more saddlers' windows, and the felt saddles that have stirrup bars. The saddle in the photograph is felt filled and should the tree break then the owner merely has to unscrew the nails in the head. The tree in the case of this saddle has arms that reach back to where the flap meets the seat, the seat having no tree, thereby reducing the risk of injury to the horse's back. A felt-pad saddle which adopts the swing type of stirrup bar can be seen in fig. 110; this saddle has a separate girth with sweat flaps and can be made in either children's sizes or for race exercising. Besides these two types there are also many children's pad saddles (fig. 111) filled with various materials; wool, foam or felt seem to be used, and the saddles are covered in leather, but like their big brothers they only have a metal head.

Lastly, but by no means least, we come to the felt-pad saddle (fig. 112) that many a child has learnt the rudiments of riding on in their early years, and probably the best type of saddle for the very small fat pony whose conformation makes it extremely hard to fit comfortably with a tree. Being soft, they cannot hurt the pony nor can they hurt the child, who finds the felt more comfortable and secure than the slipperiness of a leather saddle. Normally fitted with a leather handle on the pommel for the child to hold on to, they should be fitted with a "D" at the cantle to take a crupper, otherwise the saddle will ride over the pony's withers. Admittedly, they give the child little or no support, but they teach it balance in its early stages and when it has passed this stage it can have a proper saddle. The only things I have against them is, first, that the "D's" that suffice for stirrup bars (safety irons must always be used) are provided with rollers which can and do cut one's fingers when one comes to altering the stirrup leathers, as they become very sharp! The other thing is that the attached girth is so often left dirty —

* See Chapter Five fig. 185. They can also be sheepskin, besides knitted wool.

dirt of years at times – and as they very often ride into the pony's elbows, tend to rub and cause galls if one is not careful. The buckle, too, should always have a guard behind it or else it will catch and pinch the hair and skin. Besides felt, other pads of sheepskin and similar skins are to be found; but whatever they are made of they must be kept clean – a dandy brush will do the job well.

With the growing popularity of Western riding, a mention of the Western saddle (fig. 113) is in place. Made on a wooden tree, it is different from our saddles and weighs a considerable amount; another saddle akin to it is the Trooper saddle (fig. 114) now used a lot for trekking. This saddle, like the Western, has no panel, but relies on a folded blanket; grey army blankets folded in four are often used, though padded numnahs for both saddles can be obtained to go under the long wooden arms that form the tree (fig. 115) and rest along the horse's back on either side of the spine. The trekking saddle has metal hoops across the pommel and cantle from which a blocked leather seat is stretched; ordinary flaps are attached to these and a short leather girth is used on long girth straps. Having a pronounced dip to the seat, the saddle is used a lot by many trekking centres. There are, of course, other patterns of army saddles, looking far more like a proper saddle, but with the seat separate to the panel, which I believe are also used for trekking; but whatever saddle is used for trekking, care must be taken to see that they fit both rider and horse, realizing that in many cases the rider does not know how to save his horse, therefore making the need for a comfortable saddle all the more important, for in the majority of cases the rider may well have never ridden before or only very little, so the saddle is their security. With regard to the folded blanket – great care must be exercised to ensure that it is folded without any creases, and, too, is kept absolutely clean and dry, otherwise the horses and ponies who do their job so willingly, giving happiness to many, will suffer badly from the oversight.

Before leaving saddles, another type must be mentioned, though it does not really come into the book in the strict sense – the basket saddle, in which many toddlers have first become acquainted with a pony, and some invalids have been able to continue gaining the benefits of riding. The child's basket saddle is a basket chair on a pad that straps to the pony's back by means of a girth.

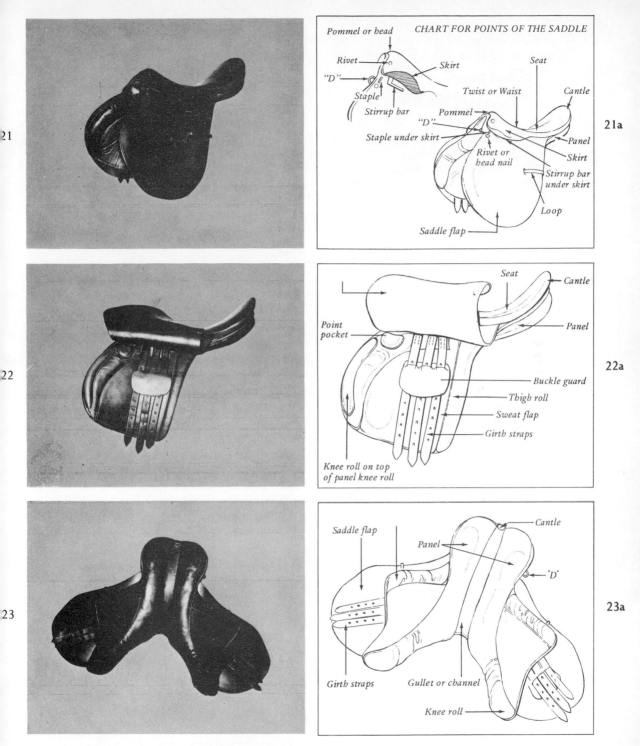

21

21a

CHART FOR POINTS OF THE SADDLE

Pommel or head
Rivet
Skirt
"D"
Staple
Stirrup bar
Seat
Twist or Waist
Cantle
Pommel
"D"
Staple under skirt
Rivet or head nail
Panel
Skirt
Stirrup bar under skirt
Loop
Saddle flap

22

22a

Seat
Cantle
Point pocket
Panel
Buckle guard
Thigh roll
Sweat flap
Girth straps
Knee roll on top of panel knee roll

23

23a

Saddle flap
Cantle
Panel
"D"
Girth straps
Gullet or channel
Knee roll

THE POINTS OF THE SADDLE

Fig. 21 and 21a: Side view.   Fig. 22 and 22a: Under the flap.   Fig. 23 and 23a: The underside.

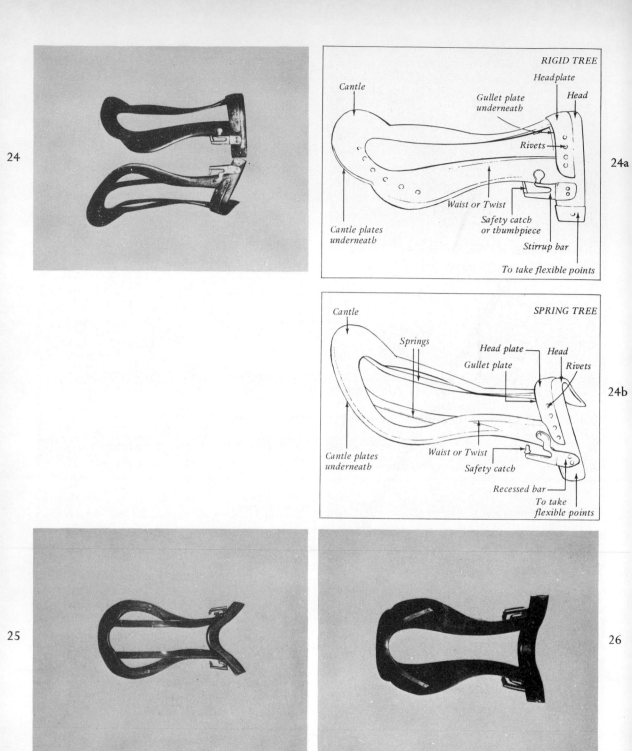

RIGID TREE

Cantle

Headplate

Gullet plate
underneath

Head

Rivets

Waist or Twist

Safety catch
or thumbpiece

Stirrup bar

Cantle plates
underneath

To take flexible points

SPRING TREE

Cantle

Springs

Head plate

Head

Gullet plate

Rivets

Waist or Twist

Safety catch

Cantle plates
underneath

Recessed bar

To take
flexible points

Fig. 24. A spring tree (bottom) and a rigid tree (top).

Fig. 25. The underside of a spring tree showing the plating.

Fig. 24a. A rigid tree. Fig. 24b. A spring tree.

Fig. 26. The underside of a rigid tree showing the plating.

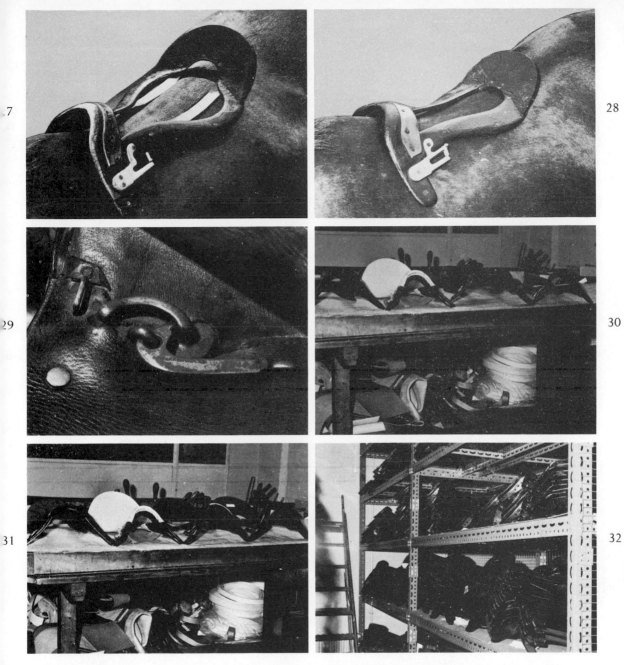

Fig. 27. The springs resting on either side of the backbone.

Fig. 28. A single rivet on a cheaper type of bar – rigid tree (158).

Fig. 29. Swing-type bar – Portsmouth Hunt Bar.

Fig. 30. Trees are made in many sizes and widths.

Fig. 31. Trees are made in many sizes and widths.

Fig. 32. Trees in the store room.

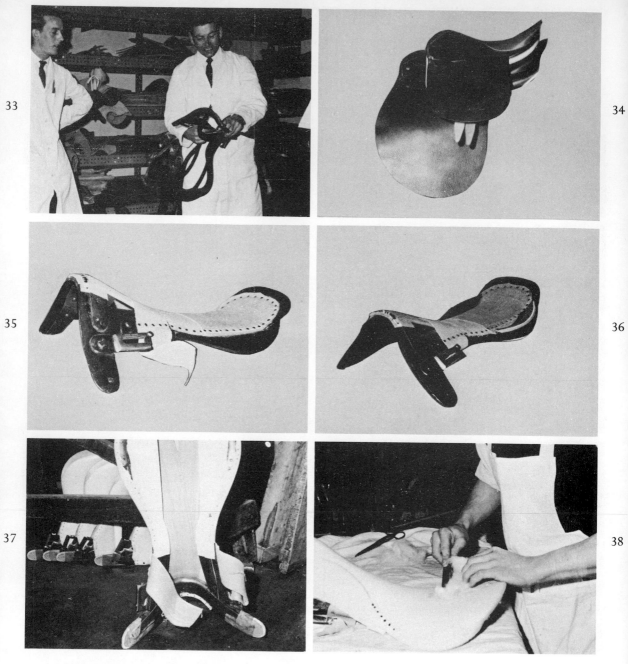

Fig. 33. An exceptionally wide tree has to be ordered specially.

Fig. 34. A tiny child's show saddle and full-sized hunting saddle.

Fig. 35. Setting up the seat – it is the whole foundation.

Fig. 36. The bellies are fitted.

Fig. 37. A spring tree with webs, flexible points and covered springs.

Fig. 38. Wool being set into the seat with a seat steel.

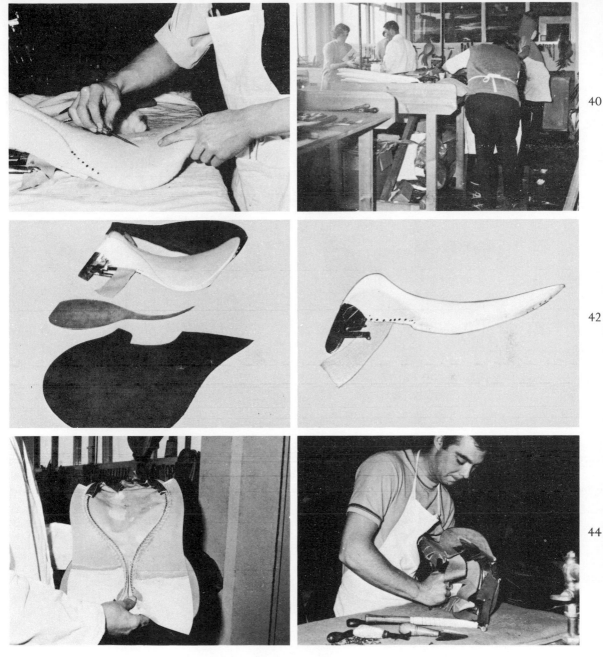

Fig. 39. Moving the wool into the required place with an awl.

Fig. 40. The saddler's shop at work – plastic foam in the foreground.

Fig. 41. A tree complete with the best-quality linen – and other parts.

Fig. 42. Plastic foam fitted over the linen.

Fig. 43. The underside view of a seat ready for fitting.

Fig. 44. Fitting the seat.

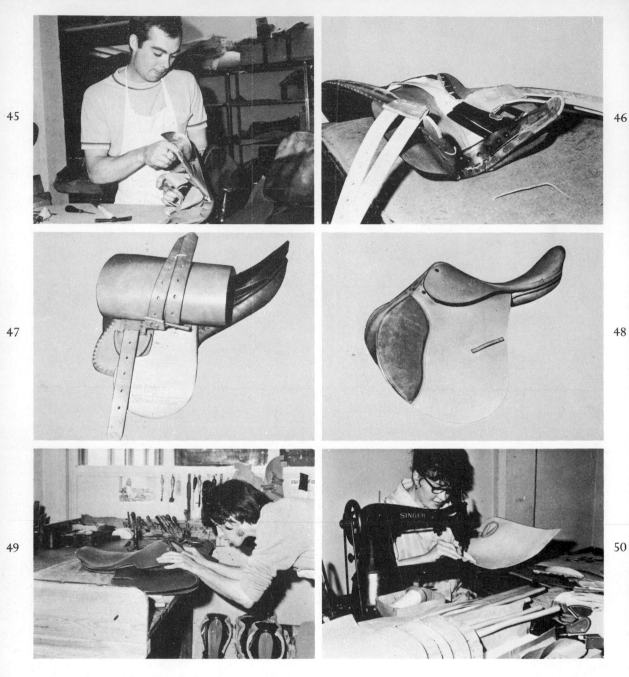

Fig. 45. Trimming the seat after it has been fitted.

Fig. 47. A special point strap (Rugby panel under flap).

Fig. 49. Ensuring the flaps are even.

Fig. 46. A saddle with chrome girth straps.

Fig. 48. Buckskin or doeskin knee grip – on a Count Toptani.

Fig. 50. Sewing on the knee rolls to the sweat flaps.

Fig. 51. Fitting a panel over the gullet lining.
Fig. 53. Saddler taking his prepared panel.
Fig. 55. The lacing nearing completion.

Fig. 52. Showing the rivets that hold on the skirt and flaps.
Fig. 54. The first stitch to lace in the panel.
Fig. 56. The final stages of lacing.

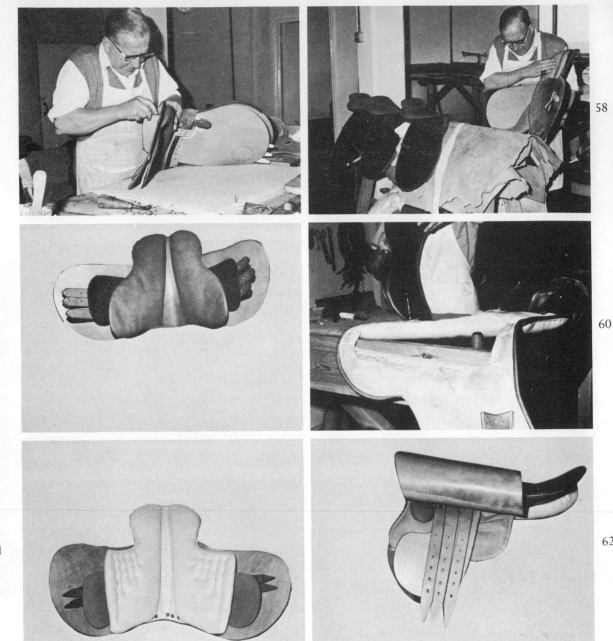

Fig. 57. Another stage in securing the panel.

Fig. 59. The underside of a Rugby panel (47 – Rugby panel under flap).

Fig. 61. A short panel serge lined (underside) – Pony Club.

Fig. 58. A job well done.

Fig. 60. A stuffed panel (short) ready for fitting.

Fig. 62. A short panel – serge lined – under the flap.

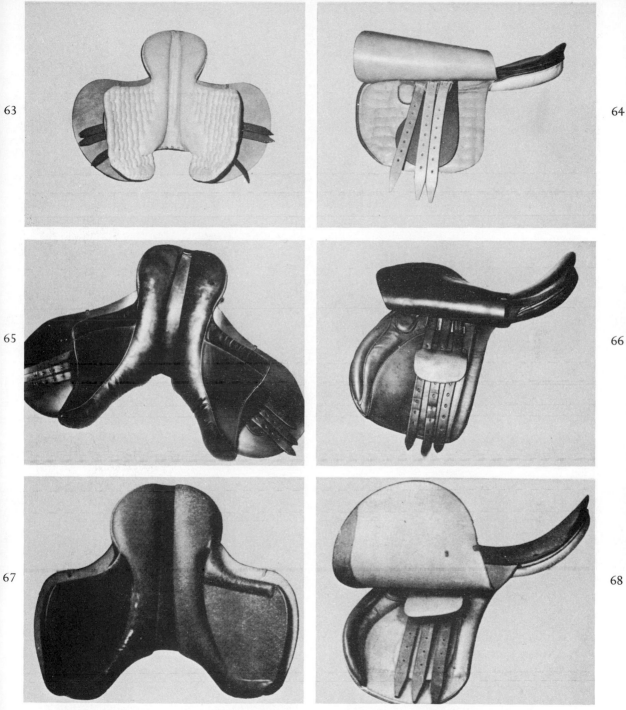

63

64

65

66

67

68

Fig. 63. A full panel – Tod Sloan flaps – serge lined (underside).

Fig. 65. Continental panel – English made – leather lined (20 and 23).

Fig. 67. An Italian-made saddle – underside – Continental panel.

Fig. 64. The same saddle under the flap.

Fig. 66. The same saddle under the flap (22).

Fig. 68. An Italian-made saddle – under the flap – Continental panel.

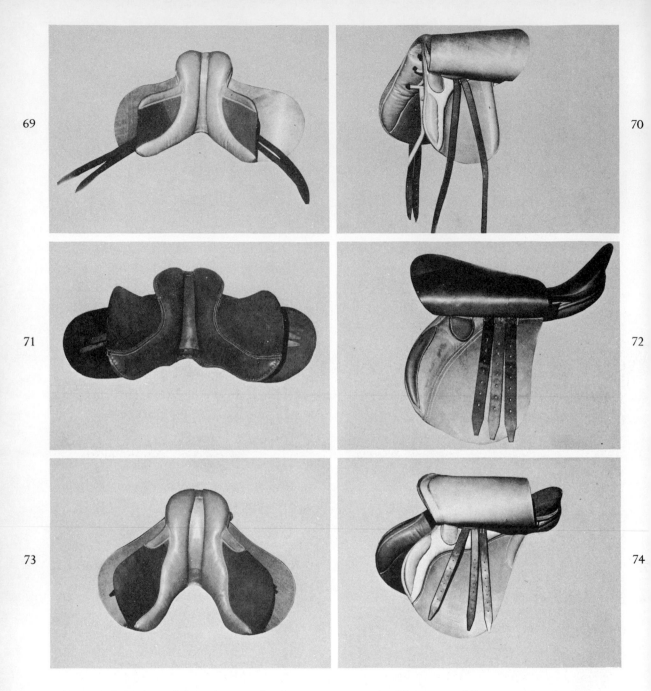

69

70

71

72

73

74

Fig. 69. Dressage saddle – long girth straps – Fulmer (underside).

Fig. 71. A stuffed Saumur panel (underside).

Fig. 73. The underside of a Saumur panel with a short thigh roll.

Fig. 70. The same saddle seen under the flap.

Fig. 72. The same saddle seen under the flap.

Fig. 74. The same saddle seen under the flap.

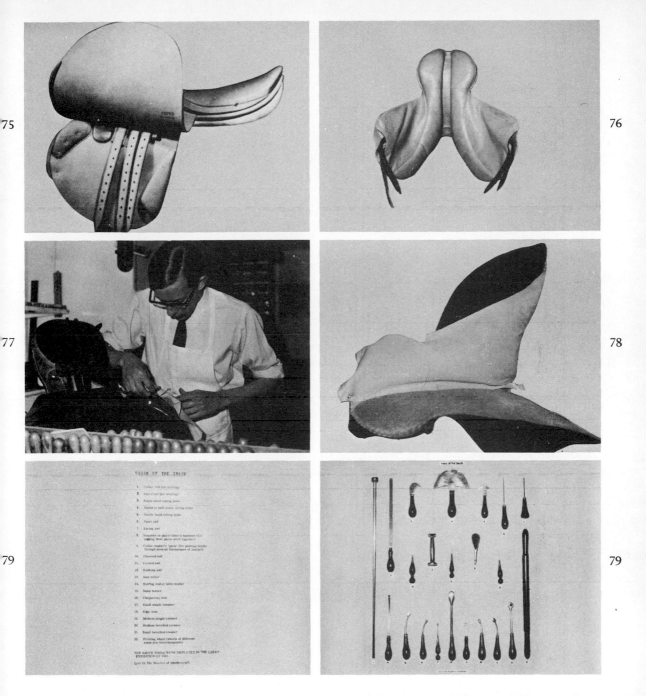

Fig. 75. Showing a thigh block on a French-made saddle.

Fig. 76. An All-in-One panel with long girth straps.

Fig. 77. Fitting a linen lining over serge.

Fig. 78. The linen lining waiting to be stitched.

Fig. 79. Saddler's tools.

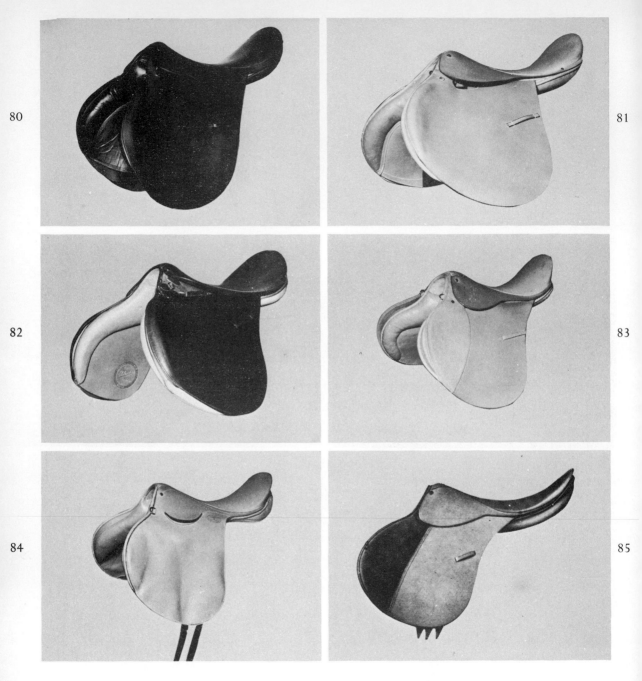

Fig. 80. Gibson All-Purpose saddle (after eight
          years' use) (21).
Fig. 82. Burghley jumping saddle.
Fig. 84. Cavalier jumping saddle.

Fig. 81. Count Toptani saddle.
Fig. 83. Milan Gold Medal jumping saddle.
Fig. 85. Milano Pariani jumping saddle.

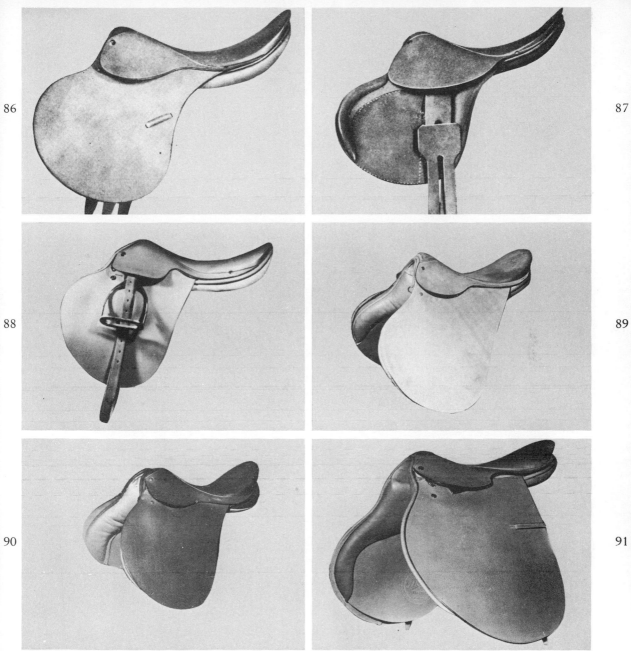

Fig. 86. Pariani jumping saddle.
Fig. 88. French-made jumping saddle.
Fig. 90. Club saddle – General Purpose.

Fig. 87. Pariani Olympic saddle.
Fig. 89. Invicta Cross-Country saddle.
Fig. 91. Beaufort General Purpose (the one being made).

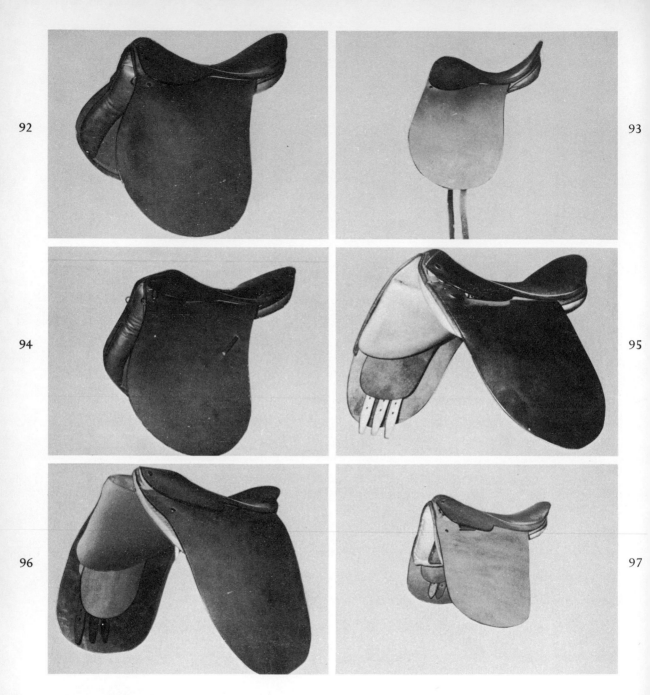

Fig. 92. Modern hunting.

Fig. 94. Dressage saddle – half cut back head.

Fig. 96. Lane Fox American show saddle.

Fig. 93. Fulmer Dressage.

Fig. 95. Show saddle.

Fig. 97. Child's show saddle.

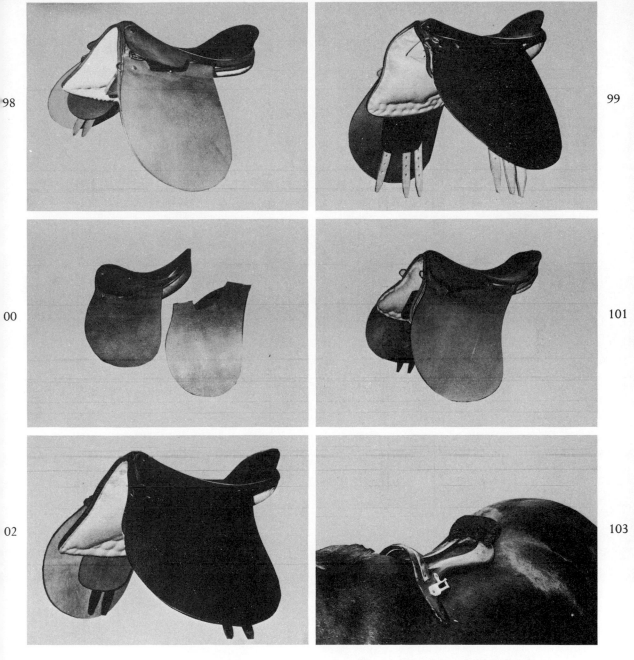

98

99

00

101

02

103

Fig. 98. School or children's saddle – serge
      lined.
Fig. 100. Child's Cadet saddle with extra pair of
      flaps.
Fig. 102. Eldonian Pony Club saddle.

Fig. 99. School saddle – leather lined.
Fig. 101. Barnsby Pony Club saddle (original
      pattern).
Fig. 103. Pony Club tree (160).

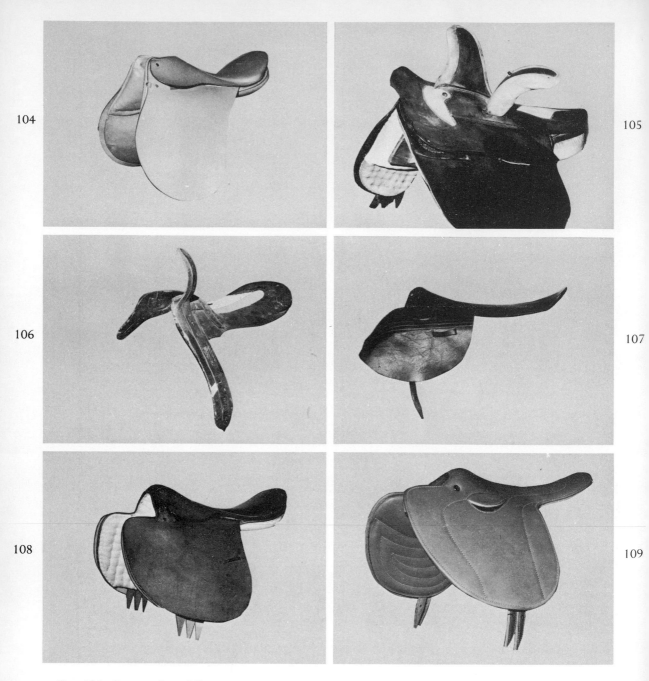

Fig. 104. Owen polo saddle.
Fig. 106. Side-saddle tree.
Fig. 108. Steeplechase saddle.

Fig. 105. Side-saddle.
Fig. 107. Flat-race saddle – minus panel.
Fig. 109. Half-tree exercise race pad saddle (Tod Sloan flaps).

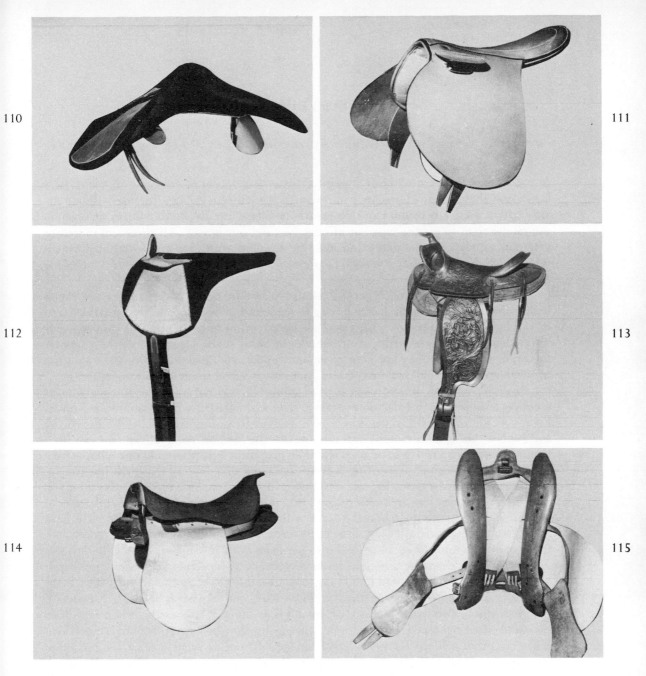

Fig. 110. Felt saddle.
Fig. 112. Child's felt pad saddle.
Fig. 114. Trooper saddle now used for trekking.

Fig. 111. Child's leather pad saddle – Cliff.
Fig. 113. Western saddle – made in Chattanooga,
        Tennessee, U.S.A.
Fig. 115. The underside of the Trooper saddle.

CHAPTER FOUR

No saddle can be used without a girth of some description to retain it on the horse's back; and though many horsemen and women are efficient enough to ride without the aid of stirrups, leathers and irons do greatly facilitate our ability to remain securely in the saddle so as to get the best out of ourselves and our horses. All three are therefore essential adjuncts to the saddle and must be selected with care and forethought as to which branch of equitation we wish to partake in, for they vary considerably according to the branch chosen.

Girths, whose principal object is to secure the saddle in the correct place and retain it there without slipping or rubbing, can be made out of several different materials and in varying designs, many of which pay special attention to prevention of chafing. Our safety depends on these girths, so it behoves us at all times, regardless of their type or material, to see that they are kept clean and supple, and in serviceable, safe condition to withstand the considerable stress and strain imposed on them by a horse in action.

Leather; woollen, union (cotton/wool mixture), and cotton — the three grades of webbing; lampwick; tubular web; string; nylon and elastic — both as ends and on its own — are all found, with sheepskin used as an oversleeve to prevent chafing. Polythene and rubber tubing are also used in this context — the former, being cheap (the required length is cut from a roll) can be used and then promptly burnt — should one's horse have some skin infection, so preventing it from spreading or infecting the girth itself.

Regardless of the type of girth, two things must be remembered — firstly, the girth must be the correct length, and secondly, that it must be the right width for the size of the horse. Too long a girth and the rider will find not only that the buckles will have moved up too high under his leg, so as to be uncomfortable, but also that the saddle runs the risk of becoming loose after the horse has been out a few hours, especially during a day's hunting or eventing, when the horse is called on to work hard. On the other hand, too short a girth, and one will find it almost impossible to do up the girth to start with, especially if the horse is one inclined to blow itself out when first saddled. It is best if the girth reaches on to the bottom or second hole on each side easily, when first done up — and when tightened, comes about half-way up the girth strap, leaving at least two holes on either side for further adjustment, as this will be needed once the horse has been out a while. As for width — the wider the girth, the larger the horse. A narrow girth would cut into a big horse and not afford the security needed; whereas a wide girth on a small horse or pony would merely cause the girth to move into the elbows and then chafe, for too wide a girth in this case would probably roll at the edges so as to rub the thin, sensitive skin in this area, till it is sore and raw.

Like with a panel lining, leather makes a good, strong girth that is safe, and providing it is cared for and never allowed to become hard and dirty is a sound investment. The only thing against leather girth is that, in summer, they can be hot, and on a soft horse up from grass, unless care is taken to check it at the first sign of trouble, chafe. Nevertheless, they are excellent girths and very hard to beat. The best known is probably the Three Fold — a widely used girth made of baghide (hide of strength and suppleness, with a special, characteristic grain embossed on it) folded into three with a piece of serge lining the centre to hold oil (neatsfoot or Kocholine) and having two buckles at each end (fig. 116); the rounded edge is worn next to the horse's elbows with the raw edge on the outside facing to the rear — otherwise it will rub, so often one sees them on back to front. In the forefront of fig. 117 on the right are several Three Fold girths in the making, both before having the buckles fitted and with the buckles waiting to be sewn on. Another well-known girth of great merit is the Balding (fig. 118), called after William Balding of Rugby, the well-known polo player; it is a plain hide girth so designed as to leave ample room for the horse's elbow to move freely without risk of chafing. Also designed with this aim in view — the Atherstone (fig. 119), showing it made with elastic ends, which is often done to enable the horse to expand his ribs fully, and fig. 120 where we have an ordinary one seen from the side that goes next to the horse's coat. Made of baghide, it is cut so as to taper in at the elbows and widen out at both ends and the middle, being joined down the centre by a strip of plain hide. A truly excellent girth, it is probably the best of the lot. Fig. 121 shows a certain number of these girths finished, lying on the bottom shelf, while above them is a pile of the thin foam strips that this firm are now inserting in the centre; serge is otherwise laid down the centre, the same as with a Three Fold, to retain nourishment for the leather and prevent it from becoming hard and drying out. These elastic ends are found on many different types of girths — not only leather ones — and on some horses are very useful. They are used in racing a lot and where a horse is called on to exert itself. Care must be taken to ensure that they are in a safe condition, for they will need renewing at intervals. Though not seen now so much, but no doubt still around in many of the older tack rooms, the polo girth (a double girth of two different widths, the narrower lying on top of the other and passing through two loops on the under one and employing a single buckle on each end) and the Military girth (a plain piece of hide with two buckles at each end and the centre section split into strips to help it grip) are both worth a mention.

Leaving those girths most commonly found in one material, we pass to those made out of more than one. The Fitzwilliam (fig. 122) is made both out of baghide with a plain hide overlay girth and in web. A good strong girth for a big horse, they are used a lot on side-saddles. The Humane girth is another that comes in leather or web (fig. 123). In this case we have a girth destined for the American market and I have turned it on its back to show the pimple rubber on its inside. These girths are used as show girths, and we can see how they are made in the following photographs. In fig. 124 we have the ends being made — this lad had just left school and joined the firm, an example that the trade is attracting many young lads on leaving school (for those who are good with their hands it is a rewarding craft) — while in fig. 125 they have been passed through the special ring (see right of photograph next to wireless) and are then sewn on by hand. Fig. 126 shows a close-up of two of these girths with some finished ones in the background. The object of these ends is to let the girth adjust itself to the shape of the horse – some horses need a longer girth on one strap than the other. The main snag against these girths is the bulk under the rider's leg, which I feel must be an encumbrance that is not outweighed by its merits.

Turning to the other materials, one very popular girth, especially with show ponies, is the tubular web show girth (fig. 127) made of two narrow webs overlapping at the centre and faced on the inside with pimple rubber, as can be seen, for I have turned the girth so that the rubber shows on the top and both sides of the buckles can be seen. A very neat girth, it does look very smart, though it is a show girth and too narrow for everyday use. Another tubular web girth is the Lampwick one (fig. 128) – cool in summer, it is soft and very strong. It is a good width and has a great deal to commend it. They wash well, though they take time to dry, which is why they are not serviceable really as a hunting girth. Web girths – single girths with a buckle at each end, and worn always in pairs (except with some children's pad saddles) – are trusted friends and come in both racing widths (narrow) and ordinary, which are in three widths ranging from 3 inches to $3\frac{1}{2}$ inches, according to the size of the horse. They also come in three grades. The best woollen ones have a reasonable life if cared for, but the others have to be watched, as they can break without much warning and wear out fairly quickly in comparison to other girths. Elastic ends are often found on web girths, especially race ones (fig. 129) – fig. 130 shows a woollen race web girth; they come in various colours. The other webbing girths look just the same, but come in a greater width. The only drawback to these girths is the fact that unless kept really clean they become hard with dried sweat and the edges then cut, causing a good deal of trouble. To clean them, first brush them with a hard dandy brush; when dry and if very muddy or sweat soaked, like after racing or hunting, scrub well and dry carefully. Incidentally, the girth on the strap nearest to the horse's elbow is placed underneath and always tightened first, the second one being placed on the rear strap and tightened second; it should overlie the under girth, giving one width between the horse's legs. Failure to do this will lead to pinching of the skin and wrinkling.

Of the cheap girths – string and nylon cord girths take a great deal of beating, especially the latter (fig. 131). The nylon one has a lot to commend it. It washes easily and dries fast – can be washed every day if necessary. It does not, if kept clean, chafe – though I gather from one saddler that there has been some trouble with some nylon girths from the nylon going into tiny bobbles that rub and cause a rash; they have brought out a new type woven differently to the general run of nylon cord, which is very soft, and is a very good summer girth, allowing air to pass through the strands to the horse's skin underneath. The quality of these girths – string is now replaced largely by nylon – varies considerably and they must be chosen with great care. Many are made of very thin strands and these will cut – pick a girth of reasonable width – not too narrow nor too wide, for they vary a lot, which is made out of nylon cord of a thick diameter and soft to handle. Recently I have used one hunting as well as hacking and showing, for it suited Castania and did not chafe her as a leather one was inclined to do. I have only two things against it. One, the buckles are always clumsy. They are made in nine cases out of ten with a roller round the top; this will not only cut your girth straps on the saddle, but also your own fingers (they are useless and should be removed before using the girth, besides they increase the bulk – why they are put on I know not.) Secondly, leaving aside the white ones and maybe the brown, these girths come in the most awful colours – bright reds, blues, yellows and greens. I know they sell like hot cakes, and how I hate to see them, for nothing looks more unworkmanlike than a garish colour. The web girths come in quiet colours that give no one any offence.

Elastic girths have proved very successful in the racing world, as they allow the horse to expand fully, but they are not for everyday use.

Though not a girth, webbing or elastic or elastic ended, surcingles have their place here, for they are used with racing saddles and over show jumping and eventing saddles. Whatever your girth you must use a surcingle to match, i.e. an elastic-ended girth must have an elastic-ended surcingle.

We now come to a specialist girth that I have kept to last, as it is only for use with a saddle carrying long girth straps – the Lonsdale, called so because Lord Lonsdale favoured them at the end of the last century. They also go by other names, such as short or belly girth. Wider than normal, they must always have a buckle protector to prevent the skin being chafed or pinched, and come either in threefold leather or special nylon cord (figs. 132 and 133), and sometimes Lampwick. The Fulmer dressage saddle and the All-in-One panel type both use these short girths.

So much for girths; no doubt there are some more, and other materials have been used and will be used from time to time, but these are a fair selection of those in use today.

Turning now to stirrup leathers – these have to be extremely strong, for we put a considerable weight on them from time to time, and the sudden stress and strain can snap them unless top-quality leather is used in making and then cared for carefully so as to maintain them in sound condition. They vary in width, ranging from $\frac{1}{8}$ to $1\frac{3}{8}$ inch, according to whether they are going to be used for a small child or a large man. Racing leathers come narrower still. Inch-wide leathers are about normal for an ordinary-sized woman of average weight, with the wider ones for extra heavy men, as they have to have a strong leather capable of bearing their weight. In the case of buffalo-hide leathers they are so strong that they can be used in a narrower width and still give the required strength. All leathers will be found to stretch with wear, and this applies in particular to rawhide and buffalo-hide leathers; so it is unwise to ride in say a point-to-point with a pair of new leathers, as by the end of the trip the rider will discover he is faced with riding far longer than he is either accustomed or wishes to, just when he and his horse are tiring and need to help each other all they can. After a time most leathers – buffalo hide excepted – will be found to have worn where they pass through the eye of the iron, so it is wise to have them shortened to change the point of wear; this is done by shifting the buckle. We have already seen how the leather destined for stirrup leathers has undergone extra greasing to ensure it is very strong. Strength is the keynote the whole time with leathers; for this reason they are always made out of leather with plenty of substance. Another point has to be observed, and that is that the leather fits the eye of the iron, for too narrow and the iron will never hang true, being continually slipping from side to side and flying off one's boot just at the wrong moment; this can be dangerous and anyway extremely vexing. Too wide and it will be impossible to put the leather through the eye without forcing it, when it will be so tight that once mounted one cannot alter the length of one's leathers.

If one looks at the end of a pair of stirrup leathers one will notice that the holes are marked (fig. 134); this is to help us adjust them to the same length on each side. Sometimes the holes are closer together; these are termed half-holes and allow the rider to get a more accurate length instead of being forced to ride too long or too short for comfort. Sometimes it is necessary to punch more holes above those already provided; a saddler will do this accurately and quickly for one. Few riders actually ride with equal weight on both irons, so it is as well to swop the leathers over from side to side; in this way one can keep them the same length.

Stirrup leathers are made from either cowhide (fig. 135) that has been specially tanned (oak bark tanned was often found to be stamped on these leathers and denoted leathers of good quality); rawhide (which is cowhide that has undergone special treatment – it is, in fact, split rawhide and has been subjected to a special vegetable tanning which leaves it recognizable by the fact that through the centre is a layer of hide that has not been tanned and is therefore, if viewed from the side, of a lighter colour than the rest of the leather – it is extremely strong); and buffalo hide (fig. 136), known also as red leather, and favoured for its exceptional strength, coupled with longevity. When a rider refers to unbreakable leathers, these are the ones he means. If one looks at a pair of stirrup leathers it is normally the grain side that has been turned in to take the friction of the eye of the iron – the flesh side being on the outside. In the case of buffalo hide leathers, it is reversed, the flesh side being so strong it does not matter. Besides these three types of leathers, it is also possible to buy Helvetia lined leathers (fig. 137). These, though expensive are excellent, for they do not stretch as much as either rawhide or buffalo, but are extremely tough and look very nice. If one looks carefully at the photograph of these leathers, we can see how the Helvetia – an exceptionally greasy leather of a yellow colour and great toughness – is stitched on to the back of the other leather to reinforce it. For those who cannot reach the stirrup iron from the ground there is an extending stirrup leather (fig. 138) which unhooks and lets down about 6 inches on strong webbing to enable the rider to reach it; once in the saddle it is hooked up again. The extending leather is always used on the nearside (or whichever side the rider normally mounts from – some people do mount from the offside, though this is not common). Personally, the only thing against these leathers is that, having let down the leather so as to reach it, one is then faced when one has mounted so far with the problem of being too low to swing one's leg over the cantle of the saddle; for this reason I hate letting down a leather when I cannot reach – I am always far worse off, neither up nor down! Some people may get on all right with them, but before expending the extra money on a pair it would be wise to try letting one's own leather down the same amount and seeing if one can reach to swing one's leg over the cantle without kicking the horse. Too, there is the risk that the leather might come unhooked at the wrong moment, leaving the rider with far too long a leather. The idea is excellent, but I feel there are definite limitations to their use.

Turning now to racing leathers – these have to be both strong and light, and bear the jockey's weight when he stands up in them. For this reason some leathers are in fact webs – that is tubular webbing, either on its own or covered on either side by chrome leather. In the case of the plain webs the points with the holes are reinforced. In either case their width is no more than $\frac{1}{2}$ inch for flat racing and $\frac{5}{8}$ to $\frac{3}{4}$ inch for steeplechasing.

According to *Summerhay's Encyclopaedia for Horsemen*, stirrup irons derive their name from the word Stigan to mount and Rap meaning rope; and can either be of metal or wood – the latter carved as in Western ones. We are concerned, though, with metal irons that start life the same way as bits. In *Bit by Bit* one can be seen on the banding machine in fig. 18. The same metals are used, namely stainless steel (the best); nickel (not very good except for children's irons, as they are liable to crack and need watching) a branded nickel mixture (these are sound and good – next to stainless steel they are the most reliable but cheaper); aluminum (used for very light racing irons and quite unsuitable for ordinary riding). In the old days plain steel was favoured, but like steel bits they had to be cleaned and are now superseded by stainless steel.

In the past there were a vast number of different types of irons, some very ornate and others of some safety pattern. Nowadays, though, the number in general use is greatly reduced and the patterns very much plainer. For ordinary riding, hunting, eventing or jumping, the so-called hunting iron (fig. 139), with its roughed tread, is the best. They normally have a rounded eye, whereas the knife-edge iron is heavier and has a square top to the eye and deepish tread with sloping edges. A good iron, but they will not take a rubber tread (fig. 140) like the Agrippin tread. These do help riders to keep their irons on their boots and the added weight helps to keep the iron hanging down and from flying off one's boot. They are excellent and a great help, being easy to take out and wash. For those who like an iron that will not rub the instep – if one rides home, they are a great blessing – the bent-top iron (fig. 141) is very good, but the top must bend away from the rider's boot and when put on the top will bend towards the horse so that the rider takes the right-hand side in his right hand to put it on his left boot. It also helps to keep the rider's heel down though it has a straight tread. Another iron that works on the same principle, but goes further, is the Kournakoff (fig. 142) offset iron, which has the tread offset and an eye offset, too; the bent-top iron has a central eye, whereas the Kournakoff's eye is angled towards the inside, so making the rider keep not only his heel down but also his foot up on the outside so that his grip is increased by forcing his knee and thigh into the saddle. This type of iron is very good for jumping, but not so suitable for ordinary riding, or dressage, as they are too restricting. Normally marked left and right, care must be taken to ensure they are on the right side and the correct way round – otherwise the rider will find himself unable to put his foot properly in the iron, or if he manages to it will be twisted in all the wrong direction.

The best known of the safety irons is one called Peacock – easily recognizable by its rubber band on the outside (fig. 143). Care is essential here, as one must ensure that the rubber band is on the *outside*, otherwise in event of the rider coming off they will not work, for they are designed so that the rider's foot, on coming into contact with the outside arm of the iron, releases the rubber band and falls clear through the gap so formed; if the other way round, the rider's foot then comes against the solid part of the iron and he might as well have an ordinary pair. When correctly put on the rubber band should be next to the horse's shoulder, the solid part being taken in the rider's right hand when mounting to place it on the left foot. They are essential for children's riding pad saddles that are fitted with a "D" in place of a safety bar. The only snag with these irons is that they are inclined to bend under the rider's weight when he mounts, so pressing down the outside of the iron; should this happen, then the rider will find his knee and thigh thrown off the saddle instead of being pressed against it as it should be for proper grip. Another form of safety iron which is meant to be good is the Australian Simplex pattern safety iron – odd looking, the other arm of the iron is so angled that it bulges forward, joining the tread on front edge. These are about the only remaining members of a family of considerable size; in the old days there were many patent safety irons and some may still be found in old-established saddle rooms.

Racing irons are light and small in comparison with ordinary irons, weighing only a matter of ounces, the usual shape being that known as cradle irons, and they can have either open (fig. 144) or closed (fig. 145) bottoms though fig. 146 is another pattern. Steeplechasing irons (fig. 147) are a heavier edition of the flat-race ones. Aluminium (fig. 148), which is very light and though to look at seems heavier than stainless steel, is on handling considerably lighter. For exercising a lighter edition of a hunting iron is used by some stables (fig. 149). Cradle racing irons are not suitable as children's irons; they only get them into bad habits and spoil their riding.

Side-saddles have their own irons, which can have a variety of shapes to the treads; the best known of the present-day ones, regardless of the tread, is either the straight (fig. 150) or offset (fig. 151) iron, and they come singly and not in pairs. The old slipper iron or cradle iron is seldom seen these days and the many patented safety irons have faded out, too, though no doubt they are to be found in a few saddle rooms.

As for the size of irons, care must be taken, like everything else connected with riding, to see that they fit the foot. Too large and one's foot could slip through, causing a serious accident if the rider was dragged – too small and the rider's foot may well get trapped if he falls. In the former case children are especially prone to having their small feet go right through the iron if they are using adult irons. About two fingers' clearance on the side of one's boot is a fairly good guide as to size – in other words at least an inch. Irons come in anything up to nine different sizes, ranging from tiny children's irons of $3\frac{1}{2}$ inches across the tread, through the quarter inches, to $5\frac{1}{2}$ inches in the case of hunting irons. Many of the other types come in fewer sizes from 4 inches up to 5 inches, the latter being normal these days for a man, while $4\frac{1}{2}$ inches to $4\frac{3}{4}$ inches for a woman – though one's boots are the deciding factor.

Besides girths, stirrup leathers and irons, breast-plates and girths are also often required to prevent the saddle slipping too far back. Some horses, either through their conformation or because they run up light in work, will "jump" through their girths, and in consequence their saddle is left behind; these horses must have some form of breast-plate to prevent this happening, especially if they are to be ridden in hilly country like Exmoor, or hunted, evented, jumped or raced under normal conditions, for nothing is more disconcerting than to find one's saddle has left its correct place and finished up somewhere in the region of the loins. The true breast-plate is made of leather and comes in various widths — hunting ones (fig. 152) being heavier than those used for steeplechasing. Should a standing or running martingale be needed with a breast-plate, then they can be buckled on to the breast ring of the breast-plate, which is very useful; in any case to prevent the horse being rubbed the breast-plate should always have a leather safe behind the ring. To attach the breast-plate to the saddle, pass the straps on either side of the withers, through either the staples — the square-headed "D" or hinged "D" which is riveted on to the tree itself, or the "D"'s on the front of the saddle just below them — then buckle to the right tension. The single strap passes through the horse's front legs and attaches to the girth. Sheepskin is sometimes needed to pad the strap that goes over the withers and the leather safe behind the big ring, should they be found to rub through friction. Sometimes the long neck straps down the shoulders are made of rounded leather, which is made by running the leather of the required width through a special gauge (fig. 153). Of the breast girths — the Aintree is probably the most seen these days, as it is used not only for racing, its original object, but also for eventing and jumping, besides hunting sometimes. Made of web (fig. 154), it is fastened under the saddle flaps to the girth above the buckle — that is, on the girth straps. In fitting this type particular care must be taken to ensure that the webbing strap does not interfere with the horse's neck and windpipe — it must come across the horse's chest just above the point of the shoulder. The elastic version is similar to the webbing one. Akin to this is the polo breast-plate, which is made of leather and has a loop stitched inside the centre of the neck to carry a martingale.

Lastly we come to cruppers (fig. 155); these are attached to the "D" in the centre of the cantle on a child's saddle or pad and the object is to prevent the saddle slipping up the pony's neck when it has little or no withers — the rounded and padded loop goes under the pony tail round its dock. It must be kept clean and well oiled, so as to be soft and supple.

Whether it is girths, stirrup leathers or breast-plates, it is essential to make sure they are fitted with good-quality buckles and on no account cheap ones, for not only will they be safer but they will not damage one's expensive saddles and accessories.

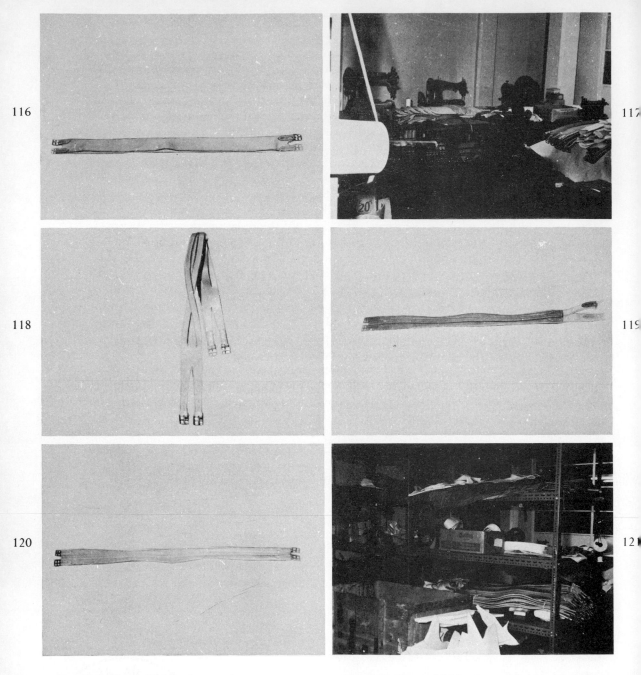

Fig. 116. Three-fold leather girth.
Fig. 118. Balding girth.
Fig. 120. Atherstone girth showing the side that goes next to the skin.

Fig. 117. Three-fold leather girths in the making.
Fig. 119. Elastic-ended Atherstone girth.
Fig. 121. Some finished Atherstone girths and foam for lining.

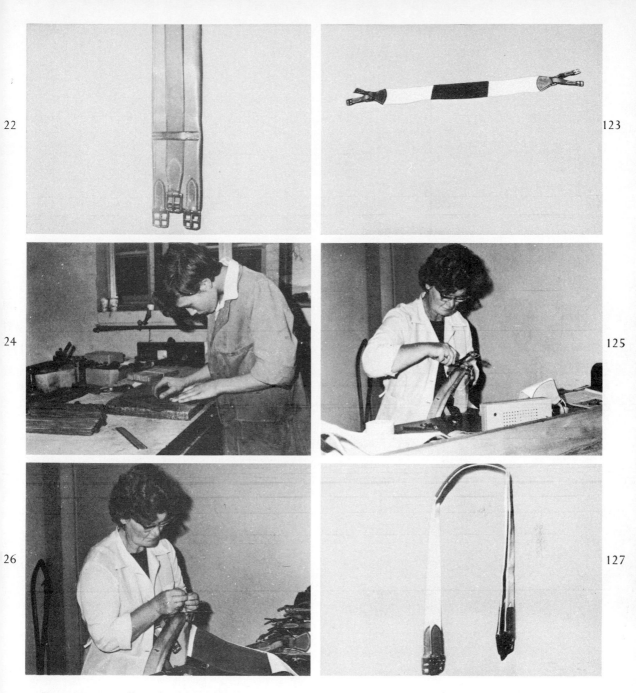

Fig. 122. Fitzwilliam leather girth.
Fig. 124. Marking out the stitch holes for Humane girth ends.
Fig. 126. Making a Humane girth in white web.

Fig. 123. Humane web girth – seen from inside.
Fig. 125. Making a Humane girth in white web.
Fig. 127. Show girth in white tubular web with pimple rubber.

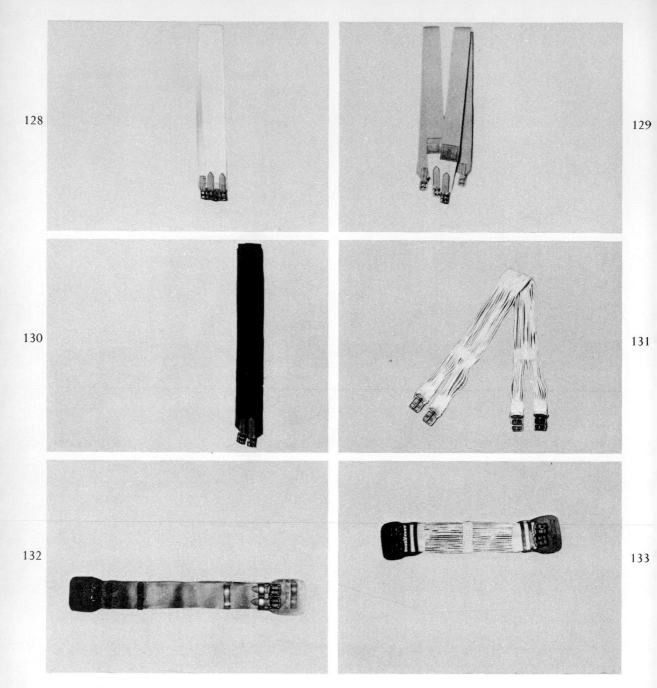

Fig. 128. Lampwick girth.
Fig. 130. Woollen web race girths.
Fig. 132. Lonsdale girth – three-fold leather.

Fig. 129. Elastic-ended web race girths.
Fig. 131. Nylon cord girth – with buckle roller.
Fig. 133. Lonsdale girth – special nylon cord.

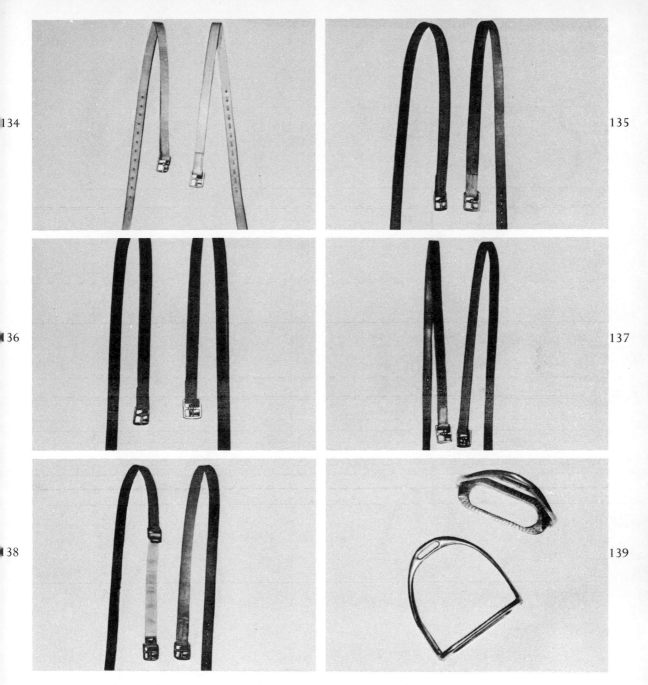

134

135

136

137

138

139

Fig. 134. Hole numbers on stirrup leathers
           (children's size).
Fig. 136. Buffalo leathers.
Fig. 138. Extending leathers.

Fig. 135. Hunting leathers.
Fig. 137. Helvetia leathers.
Fig. 139. Hunting irons.

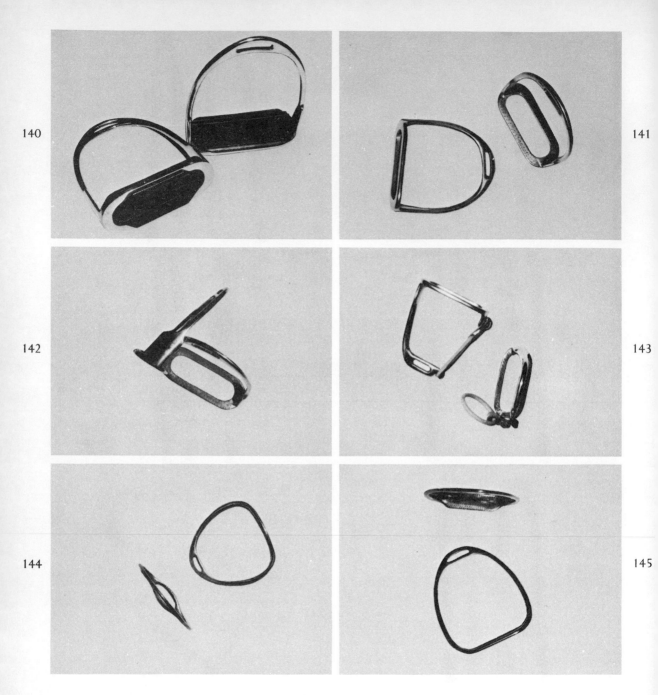

Fig. 140. Hunting irons with Agrippin treads. Fig. 141. Bent top irons.
Fig. 142. Kournakoff off-set irons. Fig. 143. Peacock safety irons.
Fig. 144. Cradle race irons – open bottoms. Fig. 145. Cradle race irons – closed bottom.

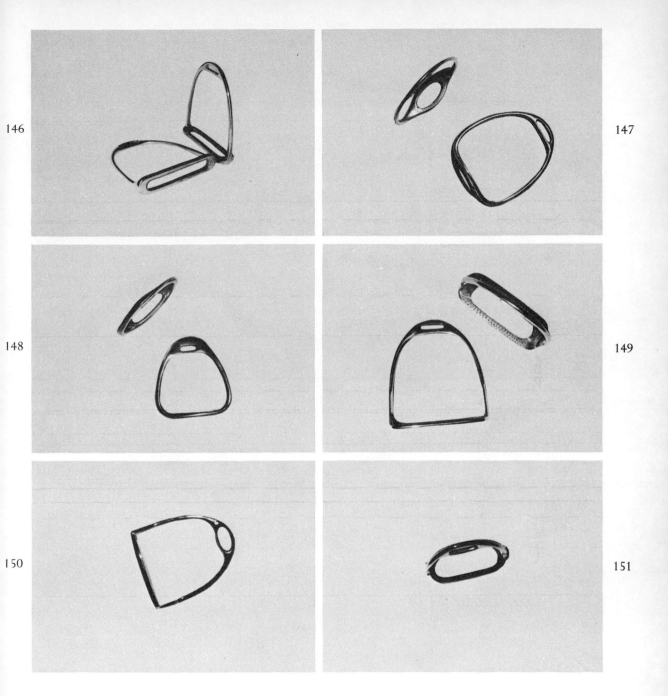

Fig. 146. Open-bottom race irons.
Fig. 148. Aluminum cradle race irons.
Fig. 150. Side-saddle iron.

Fig. 147. Steeplechasing irons – Cradle – open bottom.
Fig. 149. Race exercise irons.
Fig. 151. Side-saddle iron – offset.

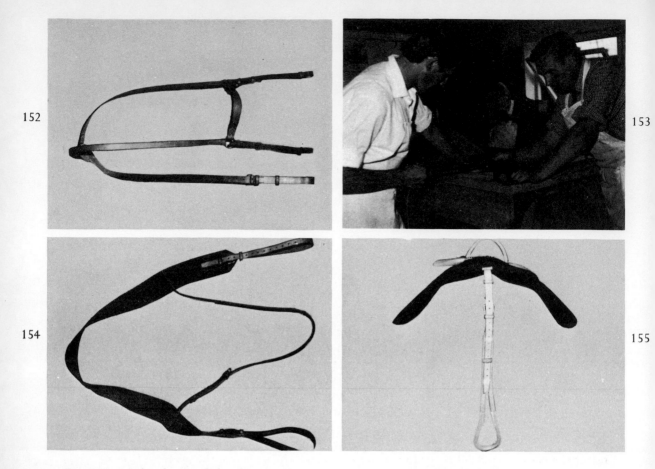

Fig. 152. Leather breast-plate – hunting.
Fig. 154. Aintree breast girth – web.

Fig. 153. Rounding leather.
Fig. 155. Crupper.

CHAPTER FIVE

AN OUTWARD GLANCE –
SADDLES AND THEIR FITTING

HOWEVER good our saddles may be they will be no earthly good unless they fit correctly. We have already seen how our horse's anatomy and our own influence the construction of a saddle; now it is time to see the part they play in saddling.

Ideally, every horse should have its own saddle, as no two horses' backs are quite alike and after a time saddles tend to settle to the outline of one particular horse's back. In the old days most horses had their own saddle stuffed to fit them; this, owing to their construction, was very necessary, as the fitting range of any one saddle was very small indeed. Nowadays, with the modern spring tree, whose head is sloping and the points flexible, this is not quite so imperative as it was, for they fit a far wider range of backs, which is a great blessing. Unfortunately it is not always possible to have a separate saddle for every horse, and, too, some riders do not always ride their own horses, but ride a variety. In which case I, personally, feel it far better to have a really good saddle of one's own that fits the rider – in my case, my saddle is so stuffed as to give my back the maximum support, for though I can still ride using a modern spring-treed saddle, I can no longer use the old type – for *providing* one's saddle fits the horse one is riding, then one is less likely to cause trouble to the horse than if one used a saddle that though fitting the horse was too small or too large for oneself; the former is the greater menace. For this reason if one can only afford so much for one's saddles and one has a couple of horses of similar conformation, then it would probably be wiser to purchase one really good saddle for use on both horses, rather than buying two cheap saddles of indifferent design for the same money. As regards the terms All-Purpose and General-Purpose, these mean the pastimes for which they are suitable, not the number of horses they will fit; they come in several fittings and lengths, though thanks to their design will fit a fairly wide range of backs, which is greatly in their favour. In the case of the rider owning more than one horse and needing more than one saddle – this is often the case when it comes to exercising with both horses going out together – then one saddle should be a really good one, the one used for the longest period of time at a stretch; while the other can, providing it is in good sound condition and of sensible construction, be much cheaper – though both saddles must fit the horses they are being used on.

If we are not to find our veterinary surgeon's account mounting up unnecessarily and our horse laid up in its stable unable to be ridden, then we must observe some basic, common-sense principles as to the fitting of our saddles. In order to help us understand a little clearer these principles, I borrowed a selection of trees of various lengths and designs from the factory and brought them home in order to photograph them resting on two totally different backs. One was a chestnut 15 hands 2 inches small show hunter, Myth; while the other was a child's pony – typical of his type, standing about 12 hands – Sparky, who at the time was in by day to keep his figure within bounds! As we have already seen in the preceding chapters, the first and foremost principle governing saddling is the absolute necessity for the saddle to afford complete clearance at all times, not only across the top of the withers, but also along the whole spinal column covered by the saddle, including the part which lies beneath the cantle arch; besides also ensuring that the points of the tree in no way hamper the play of shoulder or pinch or press the sides of the withers. One must bear in mind, too, that when the rider is mounted the saddle will rest far closer to the horse's back than when there is no weight on it. Turning now to figs. 156 and 157, we have a modern 17-inch spring tree with a sloping head and flexible points (not fitted). The width of the seat is $10\frac{1}{2}$ inches. In fig. 156 it fits Myth reasonably well, though when the panel is in place it could be too narrow; whereas, with Sparky, fig. 157, the whole head is riding far too high and is too narrow – though he has rather low withers and is decidedly rotund. In both cases there is excellent clearance of the cantle arch – with these trees it is almost impossible for them to ride too low, which is one of their many blessings. As for length, it fits Myth very well, but naturally is too long for Sparky, though, owing to its shape the rider's weight is not so likely to rest on his loins as it would be if the School tree was used (figs. 158 and 159), though it is only $15\frac{1}{2}$ inches long and the same width. The cantle in both cases, should the panel lack sufficient stuffing, would, especially if the rider was too large for the saddle, press into the backbone. On Myth it is rather too short, as it does not use the available back area to its fullest advantage; for another of the governing factors in saddling is the even distribution of the rider's weight on either side of the backbone, over as large an area as possible afforded by the bearing surface of the panel, which must conform to the outline of the horse's back and be absolutely free from lumps and ridges, both within the panel and on its bearing surface (the lining), for this lies on the muscles that pack the sides of the spinal column and take the rider's weight. It might be advisable to glance back at fig. 18, which showed us the muscles, so we know which muscles we are referring to, and how they lie. In Sparky's case his back is not so short as some 12 hands ponies, so he can use a longer saddle than his shorter-backed cousins; it would depend largely, in both cases, on the size of the rider. If Myth was being ridden by a small child, then this size fitting the child would be more suitable than a larger saddle fitting Myth, but leaving the child sliding about in the "plate". Sparky's real saddle size would be nearer 14–15 inches – for saddles range from the very tiny 12-inch saddles up to 18 inches or over for full-sized ones, 18 inches being nowadays about the largest normally made for ordinary saddles. Children's saddles range from 16 inches downwards – this size upwards being looked on as adult saddles. Spring trees need not be so long – $16\frac{1}{2}$ inches being large enough for the average rider in many cases – though the tall rider will need a larger one, and one's chosen sport also governs the length, too. Nowadays, though, there are many widths to the head: narrow – one, medium or general – two (which seems to fit a large number of backs), and broad – three, seems to be the three fittings normally available.

Returning now to the two photographs (figs. 158 and 159), the head in Myth's case, thanks to the half-cut-back head and fairly short points, could, given a suitably stuffed panel, fit well; at present, though, it shows signs of riding too low, with the risk of pressing on the top of the withers when the rider is mounted; one must be able to get three fingers between the inside of the head and the top of the withers, and also the cantle (a point so often ignored as it is behind us and what the eye does not see – in other words out of sight out of mind!) once we are mounted, and this means men's fingers not those belonging to the smaller paw of a woman or child. The ideal panel allows the saddle to fit as close to the back as is safe without any risk of pressure, for an overstuffed panel is equally bad, as it will rock and in doing so will cause friction, which leads to a sore back. As far as Sparky is concerned, especially in the summer, when most ponies are far rounder than in winter, when they have normally returned to normal, it is often necessary to ignore the height of the head within reason and concentrate on the fit of the panel on either side of the withers; it could be worse, but care would have to be taken mounting, as it would probably turn round! Even so, I would have liked it a trifle wider to drop the head so that the panel would drop down further on either side of the withers; the points, though, in both cases are fitting well. For overall fit the construction of the next tree is more sensible – $\frac{1}{2}$ inch shorter – the Pony Club tree has a sloping head and the cantle does not rest nearly so close to the backbone. Though it is shorter and has much longer points, it fits Myth (fig. 160) much better – even if it is too short. From Sparky's point of view (fig. 161) the length is good, but again the head is riding too high at present; so often in the case of ponies the saddle fits in the summer (especially if it was bought in the summer) and by Christmas the saddle has dropped right down on to the withers till it is pressing. Care must also be taken in summer to ensure that the saddle, riding up in front, does not slope back and in doing so put the child on to the cantle, which is pressed into the backbone – unless it is so fat nothing could cut into it! We now arrive at what in Myth's case is the ridiculous, a $12\frac{1}{2}$ inch-tiny child's saddle tree (fig. 162) with a quarter-cut-back head. Its object is to show how the rider's weight can be concentrated in too small an area – it covers little less than that of a wide stable roller. The head, like the school one, fits reasonably well for the same reason. From Sparky's point of view (fig. 163) the points look as if they would press in – it needs to be wider; that is the difference between a sloping and a straight one; too, he could take a longer saddle, and as this one sits at present he would also benefit from a crupper to hold the saddle back, otherwise it is going straight over his withers. The length would, of course, be all right for a very tiny child.

We now come to two trees I have only put on Myth. Fig. 164 is a rigid $17\frac{1}{2}$-inch hunting tree with a straight head, designed to take flexible points. The head is too wide by the head plates and too narrow down by the points, so that it presses badly into Myth's back – this is how pinching occurs behind the shoulder. The head, too, being straight, is riding far too close for safety in all probability; the panel of course, would make a difference, but I have my doubts as to its complete safety. The rest sits nicely; compare it with the school and see the difference (fig. 158). We now come to the last one – a spring tree for a dressage saddle (fig. 165) with a half-cut-back head. Though, in fact, much narrower than the hunting one, it fits better – Myth has very good withers, nicely shaped – even so I would not use it, as he needs a wider tree than this one; with the panel in it would be too narrow and probably pinch. Again it is designed with flexible points.

So much for the basic principles of fitting – which after all is saddling; it is now time to turn to the finished saddle, and how it fits and looks, both on its own and with a rider.

This time we have two greys – Gundulf, a 16 hands 1 inch hunter, and Cloudy, a child's 14 hands pony (fig. 166). Taking the rider first, we will start with the Gibson All-Purpose saddle. A 17-inch saddle (saddles are measured from the cantle to the nail on the head), this spring-treed saddle fits me extremely well (fig. 167) – and so it should, as it is my own! When sitting normally with ordinary length leathers, the rider should have room for his or her hand behind the back, between one's backbone and the cantle of the saddle. Caroline, on the other hand, could place nearly a hand and a half behind herself (fig. 168). These two photographs are very interesting, for they bear out what I was saying in Chapter Two. Caroline at nearly twelve, stands 5 feet $2\frac{1}{2}$ inches to my 5 feet 6 inches, and rides very nearly as long as I do – a hole shorter, in fact. I am very long from my waist to my knee, which means I need a fairly long saddle, but short in comparison from my knee to my ankle; Caroline, on the other hand, is short compared to me from her waist to her knee – hence the reason her knee is higher on the flap and she has so much saddle behind her – but longer from the knee down. All the same, owing to its narrow twist and deep seat, Caroline was extremely comfortable and found she was able to get her knees into the saddle and grip – a thing she had found impossible with their old type of prewar saddle (fig. 169), even when Cloudy was narrow, as the tree and twist were so wide, which, coupled with the long rigid points to make matters worse, just forced her thighs off the saddle, leaving her no support under her knees.

With saddles of the quality of the Gibson it is extremely easy to adjust the length of one's leathers to suit one's branch of equitation, while remaining secure and comfortable. In fig. 170 I have dropped my leathers by two holes from my normal length (fig. 167) – my seat has moved forward into the centre of the saddle and my knees now grip the lower part of the flap; while in fig. 171 I have done the reverse and shortened them by two holes. My seat has in consequence moved to the rear of the saddle with my weight coming against the cantle. My knees, too, have moved up, but still have complete support. Had this been a saddle without plenty of clearance at the cantle, it would have been very dangerous; as it is, by its very construction my weight is well clear of the backbone, resting on the muscles on either side of the spinal column. Personally, I normally jump only a hole shorter than I use for hacking and ordinary riding, and a hole longer for dressage and showing – but people vary according to what is most comfortable for them.

Turning now to Cloudy, he has a fairly long back, so can be ridden in a reasonably sized saddle. My saddle (fig. 172) is not too long and would enable me to ride him, for it fits me without running the risk of my weight pressing on his backbone, as it would if I used the shorter 16-inch rigid-tree Barnsby Pony Club saddle in fig. 173. This saddle, though, owing to its design and construction, does enable me to get my knees on to the flaps in the correct place, and had it been larger would have been perfectly all right. I need a 17½-inch rigid tree; anything under brings my weight on to the cantle even at my ordinary length. A larger rider than I would have run the grave risk of placing his or her weight back in the danger zone of the loins, though my weight is within the safety limits and placed over the rib cage; nevertheless, I am far too big and heavy to ride Cloudy, who is not nearly so strongly built as Castania was; though she was the same height, she was very strong and well up to my weight for the work I asked of her. Caroline, on the other hand, at present fits the saddle (fig. 174), and found it very comfortable, especially as she was able to get her knee nicely on to the flaps, a thing with her show saddle (fig. 175) she is unable to do, though it is also a 16-inch saddle. In a few months' time, though, she will have outgrown both saddles.

We now come to the fitting of the saddle in relation to the horse. In figs. 176, 177 and 178 we have the Gibson All-Purpose on Gundulf, without a rider, while in figs. 179, 180 and 181 I am mounted. The saddle, considering it was not his own, fits Gundulf remarkably well. Some people tend to favour as little stuffing in the panel as possible, but I do like enough to keep the saddle at all times clear of the back, without being overstuffed so that it rocks. A well-fitting saddle should leave no mark, bar sweat marks, when it is removed after a day's work, on the horse's back. If the coat is rubbed and bent backwards when the saddle is removed, then the saddle is shifting under the rider – this will cause friction. I have had remarkably little trouble in this respect with this saddle; it is so well made it very seldom marks – and then not enough to matter. Any saddle, however good, will sometimes shift the hair slightly; it is the ones that rub it up and almost break it off that cause the serious trouble, and must be attended to at once. With a sloping head (fig. 176), the pommel gives far greater clearance than it would with a straight head, so they tend to look rather cocked up until the rider is mounted (fig. 179); even so, with a leather lining saddles do not sink so much under the rider's weight as they do with a serge one (fig. 182). To fit correctly a saddle should rest comfortably behind the shoulder on the back muscles, the pommel resting snugly, without any hint of pinching, on either side of the withers, just where they run into the back. Another point must be remembered, and that is when the rider puts his weight on his irons, as when galloping or jumping with his weight forward, the pommel will sink even lower than when he is sitting in the saddle, with the result that a low pommel will be even lower, in some cases to the point of pressing. A rough guide to the correct clearance is three fingers between the withers and the pommel and the same between the backbone and the cantle; this should allow a good two fingers when the rider is mounted any less is dangerous. In the case of fig. 182, the Pony Club saddle is far too wide for Cloudy, it is a 3 fitting and he needs a 2, which, as far as I can remember, is what my own saddle is. Being brand-new, the serge is stretching fast, and had it not had a sloping head, or a cut-back one, it would have been touching under my weight – I certainly could not get two fingers in between the pommel and the withers. Nor could I in the case of fig. 183, which shows the same saddle from the rear – not elegant, I know, but it illustrates a point – that point being that a large rider on too small a saddle is sure to cause trouble before long, especially if the panel lacks enough stuffing. I am sitting centrally in the saddle, but the saddle has twisted so that the nearside of the panel is resting on the backbone. In short, it constitutes a perfect recipe for a sore back. It is a sight to be seen up and down the country all too often, when an adult tries to ride a child's pony using the child's saddle. If you must ride a child's pony, then see to it that the saddle is large enough for you as well as fitting the pony – otherwise, ride bareback! Figs. 178 and 181, on the other hand, show how the modern saddle will sit up without a rider and then, with one, rest evenly on the back, spanning the spinal column with no risk of pressing. Note, too, how the cantle offers excellent support to the rider's back, compared with the one in fig. 183, which, though made with a fair dip, is not nearly so deep as the Gibson.

A look at the girths in the foregoing photographs. Gundulf has an Atherstone, which can be seen clearly in fig. 177, where it fits into the natural groove formed by the termination of the sternum bone. Cloudy, on the other hand, has either a white or brown nylon cord girth, depending on the saddle.

Should our horse need a breast-plate, then this is fitted either to the "D"s on the front of the saddle (fig. 184) or the staple, which can be seen directly above it, depending on which fits best, and the saddle, and the amount of strain imposed on it. In this case we have a race-width one – though they are also used for eventing in this width – hunting ones (fig. 152) are wider. To judge if it is large enough, pass your hand on its its side under all the straps – it should fit easily. A hand's width is also required between the windpipe and the breast ring. This one is far too short in the neck straps for Gundulf – the ring wants to drop at least 2–3 inches below his windpipe.

Sometimes the rider is faced with having to use a saddle that has insufficient clearance over the withers; the only answer in this case is to use a wither pad (fig. 185), to protect the withers from pressure until the saddle can be re-stuffed or a better one found. It is only a temporary measure. The best type are made out of knitted wool, but sheepskin is also used, and foam plastic would also be suitable. Whatever type is employed the fitting is the same – the pad must be fitted into the head so that a gap is left over the withers. It is very wrong to put them on flat and then put the saddle on on top – they only press this way. The saddle in fig. 185 is a straight-headed old prewar-type saddle and its wide seat can be clearly seen, and its long points stand off on either side of Cloudy's shoulders.

Nowadays, numnahs are seen a great deal. How good they are is a matter of opinion; some people like them, some do not. If used because the saddle does not fit, then they have a use, but only temporarily, for a numnah will not correct the fit of a saddle – the saddle itself must be stuffed to fit. All the same there are horses who like a numnah under their saddles and benefit from them – though they do add bulk between the rider and his horse's back. For these customers either a sheepskin (fig. 186), which is soft, but goes lumpy if not kept absolutely clean, or a foam numnah (fig. 187), covered in linen and quilted, are very good. Sheepskin, though, does tend to make the horse's back soft, owing to the moisture that the wool generates when the horse gets very hot, whereas the quilted foam numnahs seem to be better and are just as soft. They are not so hot and therefore do not draw the back in the same way. Sponge rubber numnahs did this and with felt ones are dying out now in favour of foam plastic ones. With the quilted ones care must be taken to see that there are no bobbles where they are quilted, as these could rub; some are stitched this way, especially the nylon or other man-made fibre covered ones, for several washable materials are now being used to cover them. The good thing about these is the fact that they wash very easily and can be kept clean and dry. Whichever type is used, the fitting is the same. They should be about an inch larger than the saddle and the centre must be pushed well up into the gullet to give the backbone clearance. In fig. 188 we have an unlined sheepskin one (fig. 186 was linen lined) – the leather strap going under the saddle flap and on to the front girth strap. Whereas in fig. 189 we have a nylon-covered foam one that is held on by a band of elastic that goes right over the top side of the panel under the flap. In this photograph a pair of web girths are being used. Lastly, we come to a very cheap and useful type of numnah – namely, plain 1-inch plastic foam cut to fit (fig. 190). Its present cost is 2s. a square yard and the piece I used under my saddle cost me under 5s. Being soft, there was no need to bring it right down under the flaps; I used it only under the seat. It is very useful indeed if your horse has a sore spot on its back and pressure must be removed. You just cut a piece out where required. The foam does not slip and remains in the right place. Castania got an infected hair root on her back and I used it for several months. To wash it just place it in hot Savlon and leave for ten minutes, then rinse out and prop up to dry. To cut it to shape just place the whole bit of plastic (obtainable from a do-it-yourself shop) on the horse's back and place the saddle on top, draw a line round with a black felt pen and then, after removing it from the horse, cut round the outline and trim off the edges. There is no need to use coloured bathmats!

However well our saddle fits it must be put on with care, for careless saddling only leads to an uncomfortable horse. If rugged, slip the rugs off over the quarters and then, taking the saddle over one's left arm (fig. 191), so that the pommel rests against one's upper arm for protection, stand against the horse's near shoulder and run your right hand along the horse's back – from the withers to the loins – to ensure the coat is lying flat and there are no lumps. Then lift the saddle with both hands and place well up on the withers, and slide gently backwards into its correct place. Going round to the offside, take the girth and attach it to the girth straps, making sure all the flaps and straps are lying flat. So often people leave the girth attached to the offside and merely fling it over from the nearside without going round; with the result that the straps and flaps are often twisted and stick into the horse. Returning to the nearside, bend down and take the girth in one's right hand – if a martingale is used or a breast-plate, slip the girth through the loop so that it lies in the centre – then fasten the girth on the nearside. One can use either the first and last strap (fig. 192) or the first and second (fig. 193), according to which fits best with one's girth, and then slide down the buckle guard to prevent the flap getting cut from the buckles. In fig. 192 Myth has an Atherstone girth fitted on to the first and last straps, while with Gundulf his threefold (note the way round it is) girth is on the first two straps – the stitching on the girth holding the second buckle needs renewing if it is not going to come undone. Girthing up should be done evenly, a hole or two on each side at a time. Once girthed up, lift the horse's fore leg and pull it gently forward (fig. 194) – first one leg and then the other – to ensure that the skin is not wrinkled or pinched under the girth. To unsaddle, run the irons up the leathers and then release the girth; if the horse is warm, only loosen it a few holes and shift the saddle to let air get under it, for it is bad to whisk a saddle straight off a hot back – it must cool off first. Having loosened the girth, place a rug over the horse's back and saddle if it is cold and leave tied up for about ten minutes, by which time the saddle can come off. Next, having undone the girth on the nearside, remove the martingale or breast-plate if worn, then place the girth over the saddle – do not leave it trailing – and lift the saddle clear, removing it well out of harm's way while the horse is re-rugged. Incidentally, many sore backs are caused by badly fitting rugs and rollers, and not by saddles, so do see that the roller is well stuffed and does not press on the top of the backbone.

In winter, with clipped horses out exercising, it is wise to place a rug under one's saddle (fig. 195). The rug is put on first and slid back into place, then the offside is folded over the withers and the nearside over that in that order; the saddle is then carefully placed on top of the rug in its correct place (do not slide it back) and girthed up. In the old days things were made to last; the rug was my mother's back in the early twenties and has been mine for the last twenty years – alas, they do not last so well today! The back of the rug is anchored by a fillet string attached to the rug on either side and passed across the horse's hocks just above them, under the tail – it prevents the rug blowing up.

In summer, when horses come up from grass, often one's girth that fits during the season is too short; at times like this a girth extension (fig. 196), is extremely useful, as it gives the much needed-extra holes.

Well, so much for saddles and their fitting. It must be remembered, though, that the horse's back *must* be hard before any real work is asked of the horse, or any saddle, however well fitting and carefully put on, will tend to cause trouble, the same way as if we go for a long walk when our feet are not used to it they blister. Also, should we have to travel with our saddle, then it is worth getting it a proper case (fig. 197), as this will prevent it from getting damaged and scratched; too, when at home placed over the saddle on its rack (closed up), it makes an excellent cover to keep off the dust and dirt.

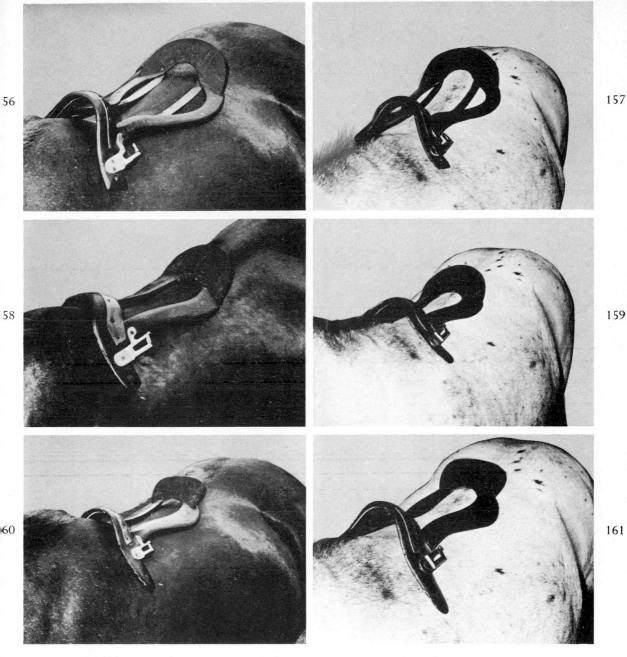

56   157

58   159

60   161

Fig. 156. Myth – 17-inch spring tree with sloping head

Fig. 158. Myth – school tree with cut-back
head – 15½-inches (28)

Fig. 160. Myth – Pony Club – 15-inch tree –
sloping head (103).

Fig. 157. Sparky – the same tree.
Fig. 159. Sparky – the same tree.
Fig. 161. Sparky – the same tree.

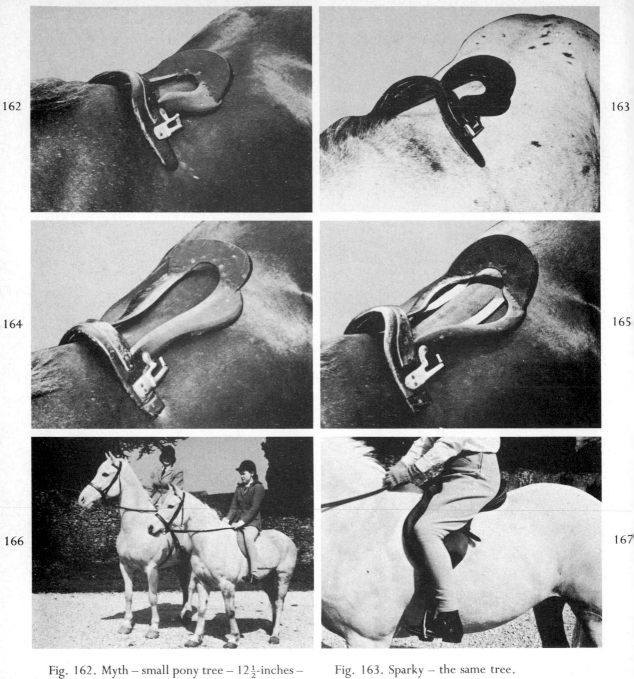

Fig. 162. Myth – small pony tree – 12½-inches – cut-back head.

Fig. 163. Sparky – the same tree.

Fig. 164. Myth – 17½-inch hunting tree – straight head.

Fig. 165. Myth – spring dressage tree – cut-back head.

Fig. 166. Gundulf – the hunter; and Cloudy – the pony.

Fig. 167. A normal-length leather on an All-Purpose – Gundulf.

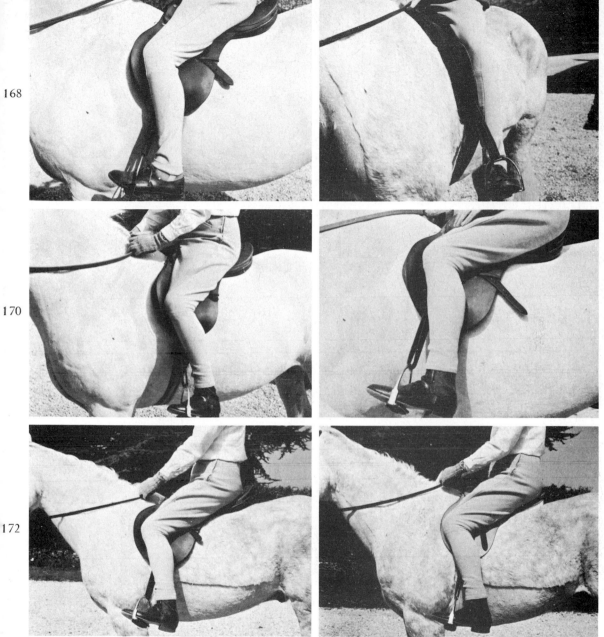

Fig. 168. Caroline on the same saddle – Gundulf.

Fig. 169. Forcing the rider's thighs off the saddle – Cloudy.

Fig. 170. Having let my leathers down two holes – Gundulf.

Fig. 171. And two holes shorter than normal – Gundulf.

Fig. 172. Cloudy with a saddle to fit the rider.

Fig. 173. A good saddle, but too small for the rider – Cloudy.

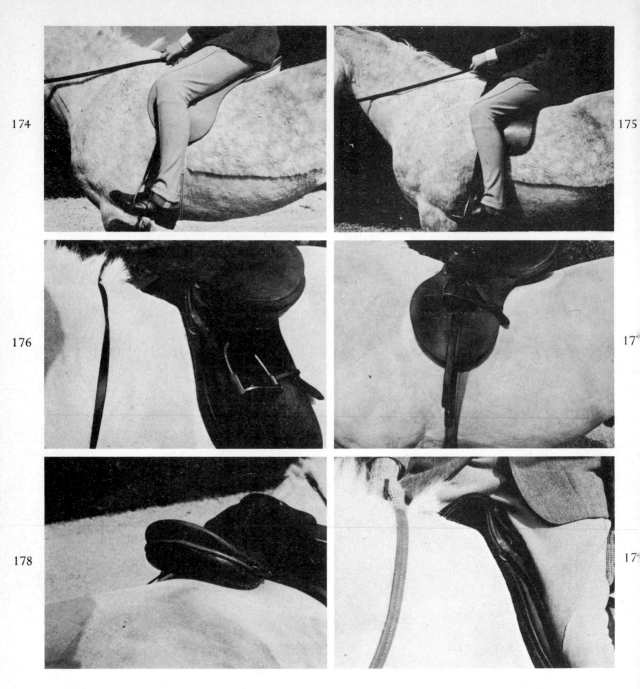

174

175

176

17

178

17

Fig. 174. Caroline on the same Pony Club saddle – Cloudy.

Fig. 176. Gundulf – Gibson All-Purpose saddle – front view.

Fig. 178. Gundulf – looking at if from behind.

Fig. 175. Caroline cannot get her knees on to the show saddle.

Fig. 177. Gundulf – a side view of the saddle.

Fig. 179. The pommel drops down under a rider's weight – Gundulf.

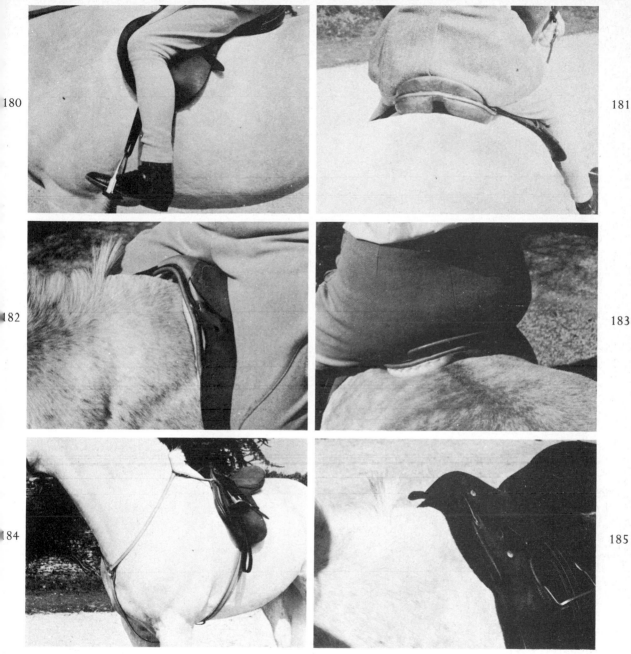

Fig. 180. The rider's weight evenly distributed
– Gundulf.

Fig. 181. Under the rider's weight the cantle
gives good clearance.

Fig. 182. The tree was too wide for Cloudy –
insufficient clearance.

Fig. 183. The perfect recipe for a sore back –
Cloudy.

Fig. 184. A race breast-plate on Gundulf – too
small.

Fig. 185. A woollen wither pad under an old-
type saddle – Cloudy.

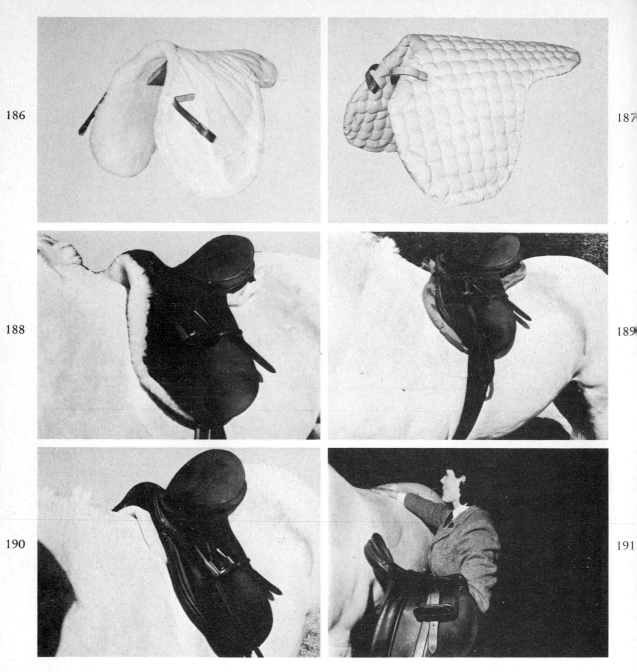

Fig. 186. A sheepskin numnah – linen lined.

Fig. 187. A linen-covered quilted-foam numnah.

Fig. 188. A sheepskin numnah under a saddle – Gundulf.

Fig. 189. A nylon covered foam numnah under a saddle – Gundulf – with a pair of web girths.

Fig. 190. One-inch plastic foam makes a good numnah.

Fig. 191. With the saddle over your left arm, run your right hand along the back.

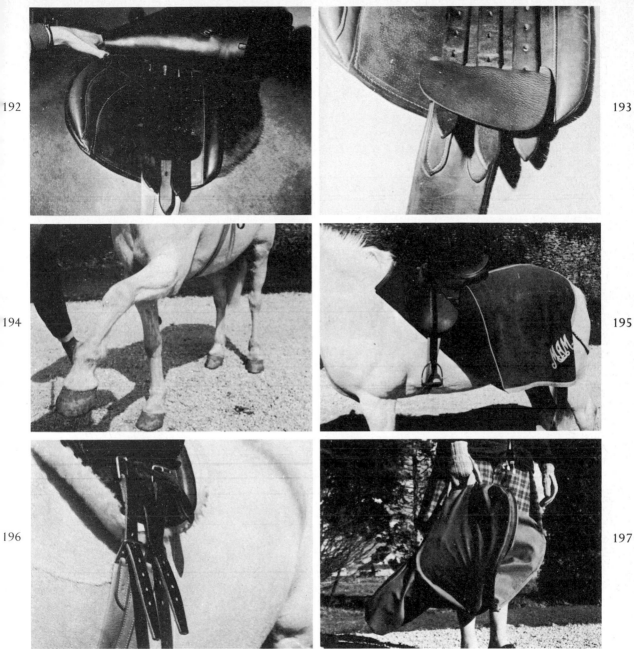

Fig. 192. Myth – Atherstone girth on first and
last strap.

Fig. 194. Having tightened the girth pull the
fore-leg forward.

Fig. 196. A girth extension is sometimes useful
– Gundulf.

Fig. 193. Gundulf – three-fold girth on first
two straps.

Fig. 195. Exercising in winter a rug is necessary.

Fig. 197. A carrying case is a great help when
travelling.

CHAPTER SIX

By and large saddle injuries are the fault of the owner, groom or rider, and therefore, except in special cases, avoidable; nevertheless, they do occur, and in really serious cases even warrant the intervention of the R.S.P.C.A., as was proved by their advertisement that appeared in the Personal Column of the *Daily Telegraph*, November 1968 (fig. 198). It is one thing, though, to say they are avoidable, but another to prevent them if one has not the necessary knowledge to do so, ignorance and carelessness being the prime causes. The latter is inexcusable, but the former can only be remedied by the acquisition of sound, reliable knowledge. Realizing this, I asked our own veterinary surgeon, who specializes in horses and has a very wide and extensive knowledge of them, for his help. The rest of this chapter is therefore based, virtually verbatim, on his notes and not drawn just from my own observations.

Saddle injuries are caused by either (1) uneven, (2) excessive, or (3) prolonged pressure and friction; or a combination of these factors. Regrettably the back of the healthy horse in good condition will tolerate considerable abuse, and a fit light-weight rider using worn-out saddlery will not cause the same damage that results from a heavy, unfit rider rolling about in the saddle.

As we have already seen in earlier chapters, the weight of the rider must be evenly distributed over the large muscles mass which covers the top of the rib cage, for the bony prominences of the spine are only covered with skin and are not adapted to withstanding pressure, particularly in the area of the withers. Injuries in this area are caused by a saddle which is too wide, allowing the channel, inside the head, to come down on the withers, producing an obvious sore. At the same time a saddle which is too small and too narrow will exert a pinching effect each side of the withers, producing an obvious pressure mark when the saddle is removed at the end of the ride, and followed by the appearance of a hot, painful swelling on each side of the withers in twelve to twenty-four hours' time. This type of bruising will produce a chronic and intractable inflammation of the spinous processes in the area of the withers if the cause is allowed to persist. This condition is almost an occupational hazard of horses which are unfortunate enough to have to carry a side-saddle.

Occasionally unreasonable pressure on the side of the withers will cause rupture of blood bessels under the covering of the back muscles with the formation of a blood clot (Haematoma) in the area. This will show as a fairly tense, sharply defined swelling about the size of half an egg, and frequently in the middle of the swelling a ring can be felt with the finger-tip – this is where the covering of the muscle has split under pressure.

In the same way that the skin of a man's hand hardens and thickens with work, so does the skin of the horse's back under the saddle. This allows the back to withstand the friction of the saddle, but the toughening process takes several weeks to develop, which is why care must be taken when riding the horse during this time. Excessive pressure or friction during this period will produce damage ranging from a slight puffiness and tenderness of the affected area to a condition where the hair has been rubbed away and the skin is moist, red, and inflamed – in severe cases the surface layer of skin may have been eroded, leaving a raw surface. Naturally prompt action must be taken and I will deal with treatment for these conditions at the end of the chapter.

Another saddle injury to which the pundits devote considerable attention is one with the common name of Sitfast. This condition is, in fact, as uncommon in these days as it is painful. It is a true corn – a hard, horny, dead circle of skin about the size of a halfpenny, usually on the side of the withers. This, like the human corn, is caused by prolonged and excessive pressure on a small area, resulting in a loss of blood supply to a circumscribed patch of skin. The resultant condition is, like its human counterpart, extremely tender and resistant to treatment.

We now come to the only saddle injuries which cannot be attributed to ignorance or carelessness, and these are those caused by either warbles or the various fungus infections. The former appear usually in March in the Northern Hemisphere, and are characterized by the sudden appearance somewhere along the back of a raised, hot, painful swelling, some 3–4 inches in diameter, and for no obvious reason. The sudden and inexplicable appearance of the typical swelling should always be followed by careful examination of the area. In the middle of the swelling there may be found a small hole through which eventually a rather puzzled cattle warble (we saw them in relation to cattle in Chapter One fig. 2) may emerge, having spent the last few months in a strange and probably hostile environment.

The most common fungus infection of the horse's back is caused by the *Sporotrichosis* group of infections. This fungus when inoculated into the skin produces hard, nodular, pea-like swellings in the skin, irregularly distributed, but usually in the area of maximum friction – the bearing surface of the saddle and along the edge of the saddle flaps. These nodules are small, hard and painless, and only cause trouble when they protrude and are rubbed. Under normal conditions of careful management they tend to be pushed back into the surface of the skin and there they remain until the pressure is released.

The second fungus infection – typical ringworm – is usually confined to the lower area of the saddle flaps and the girth, if this is the source of infection. The condition starts with the appearance of small round spots which quickly lose their hair covering and become dry, crusty, itchy, and progressively larger. If the disease is not checked at this stage and the infected area is further damaged by sweating or friction, the ringworm may become infected with secondary septic germs, producing very quickly a large, raw, suppurating area with severe skin damage and even a feverish reaction.

The treatment of saddle injuries calls for common sense on the part of the person responsible for the care of the horse, and is first directed at the removal of the cause. Stop using a particular saddle; lunge; turn out; or ride bareback. Repair; re-stuff or change unsuitable saddlery – it may be necessary to turn back the front of the night rug over the surcingle or roller to avoid pressure on the withers. Also, to avoid pressure on a certain area a numnah, either sponge (the plastic foam we saw in fig. 190 is ideal) or felt, with a hole cut out to ensure complete clearance of the trouble area, is often necessary if a saddle must be used.

In cases where there is marked inflammation, tenderness and swelling, and pain, it is usually necessary to poultice the area for several days until the swelling has subsided. The most efficient way of doing this is to apply a thick layer of warm kaolin poultice to the injury and then cover with a rug, to the underside of which has previously been stitched waterproof material and a pad of Gamgee tissue. The same technique can be used for Animalintex dressing.

As a follow-up treatment it is usually better to use a lotion, particularly of the evaporating type, rather than ointments, the aim being to dry and harden the area quickly. Of the home remedies calamine lotion is inexpensive and effective.

With regard to the treatment of serious injuries and the fungus infections, it would normally be necessary to seek veterinary advice early on. I cannot endorse this last sentence too strongly; it never pays to leave an injury of any kind that fails to respond quickly to home treatment, and serious ones if they are to be cured satisfactorily, must be tackled by a veterinary surgeon in their early stages. Normally if I cannot get satisfactory results myself within four to six days, then I find it far better to get professional help. In this way one's horse is back in action in the quickest possible time – it is well worth it.

The Daily Telegraph, Monday, November 18, 1968

PERSONAL

Private 20/- per line. Trade 40/- per line. Charity Appeals 10/- per line.

SCANDALOUS CRUELTY at RIDING SCHOOL. A Skewback mare being ridden in a gymkhana was discovered by an R.S.P.C.A. Inspector to have suppurating saddle sores. The owner, a riding school proprietress, was fined. Help the R.S.P.C.A. to prevent such cruelty by sending all you can spare to The Secretary, R.S.P.C.A., 105, Jermyn Street, London. S.W.1.

Fig. 198. Neglect of saddle injuries even warrant intervention of the R.S.P.C.A.

(*Daily Telegraph*/R.S.P.C.A.)

CONCLUSION

SADDLING, like bitting, is a complex and fascinating subject which I trust this book
has made a little clearer. For only if we study the subject in all its aspects can we hope
to understand, and without understanding we can never gain the fullest benefits from
our excellent modern saddles – and the best out of ourselves and our horses. Whatever
our pastime or branch of equitation – and however good our saddle – we will never
succeed unless we remember that our horse must be comfortable at all times; for an
uncomfortable horse is a restless horse that will never settle to the job in hand, and
will work itself into a frenzy in its efforts to down both its saddle and its rider. A horse
or pony really playing up from pain or extreme discomfort will refuse to calm down or
give in until the cause is removed or it is exhausted; whereas one playing the fool from
pure high spirits will – providing the rider can stick it out – sober up once it has had
its fun!

On the other hand, there is no better sight – or joy to ride – than a horse or pony
with a really good saddle, well cared for and comfortable for both, as these are the
things that lead to a true and wonderful partnership of horse and rider – regardless of
one's sport or pastime.

A wonderful partnership – Christmas 1966.